2021

D0423754

CULTURE SMART!

ARGENTINA

Robert Hamwee

·K·U·P·E·R·A·R·D·

This book is available for special discounts for bulk purchases for sales promotions or premiums. Special editions, including personalized covers, excerpts of existing books, and corporate imprints, can be created in large quantities for special needs.

For more information contact Kuperard publishers at the address below.

ISBN 978 1 85733 705 1
This book is also available as an e-book: eISBN 978 1 85733 706 8

British Library Cataloguing in Publication Data
A CIP catalogue entry for this book is available from the British Library

First published in Great Britain
by Kuperard, an imprint of Bravo Ltd
59 Hutton Grove, London N12 8DS
Tel: +44 (0) 20 8446 2440   Fax: +44 (0) 20 8446 2441
www.culturesmart.co.uk
Inquiries: sales@kuperard.co.uk

Series Editor Geoffrey Chesler
Design Bobby Birchall

Printed in Turkey

About the Author

ROBERT HAMWEE is a training and management consultant who was born and brought up in Argentina before moving to the UK at the age of twenty-three. He has a degree in music and business management and speaks six languages. He is currently a learning solutions lead for Accenture, and was previously founder and director of Aliquot Consulting Group, specializing in international and cross-cultural training and business issues.

The Culture Smart! series is continuing to expand.
For further information and latest titles visit
www.culturesmart.co.uk

The publishers would like to thank **CultureSmart!**Consulting for its help in researching and developing the concept for this series.

CultureSmart!Consulting creates tailor-made seminars and consultancy programs to meet a wide range of corporate, public-sector, and individual needs. Whether delivering courses on multicultural team building in the USA, preparing Chinese engineers for a posting in Europe, training call-center staff in India, or raising the awareness of police forces to the needs of diverse ethnic communities, it provides essential, practical, and powerful skills worldwide to an increasingly international workforce.

For details, visit www.culturesmartconsulting.com

CultureSmart!Consulting and **CultureSmart!** guides have both contributed to and featured regularly in the weekly travel program "Fast Track" on BBC World TV.

contents

contents

Map of Argentina

introduction

Argentina is a country that embraces much more than *gaucho*, tango, polo, and football. Very unlike its Latin American neighbors, it has evolved in a distinctive way, and is quite different from the expectations many visitors have of a stereotypical Latin American destination.

The Argentinians have developed a style, a language, and a way of life that are all their own. They are a passionate, friendly, extroverted, and, particularly in Buenos Aires, vociferous people who have experienced the hardships of cruel economic downturns and hyperinflation of gargantuan proportions. For Argentinians there have also been golden eras, when traveling abroad was commonplace and, ironically, cheaper than staying at home.

Argentinians are stylish, sophisticated, and quite homogeneous—not the multicultural society we find in many other countries. Neither very disciplined in their everyday life, nor great team players, they are, however, a nation of hardworking and resilient people whose character has been molded by external factors rather than driven by internal values.

The waves of immigrants that arrived in the twentieth century, mainly from Europe, brought with them a wealth of knowledge and culture that played a crucial role in the development of art, literature, and general lifestyle. Buenos Aires, with one of the world's largest opera houses, as well as museums and galleries, has produced writers and poets of distinction, and has gained a reputation as one of Latin America's great cultural centers.

After the Second World War, Argentina underwent a series of political upheavals, culminating in a coup in 1976 that brought one of the worst dictatorships in its history. The war with Britain in 1982 over the Falkland Islands, or Islas Malvinas, contributed to the government's own downfall and paved the way, albeit aided by a sad turn of events, for the restoration of democracy.

Still facing political and economic problems, the Argentinians today seem to have gained control of their own destiny. This, however, has been marred by a series of questionable economic policies and tense relationships with foreign investors, leading to pessimism about their government's ability to manage the ailing economy. Many look forward to policy changes in 2016 with more hope. Despite these problems, the Argentinians welcome visitors with open arms.

This book deals with the many facets of the Argentinian way of life. It has been designed to give you an insight into their social and business habits, culture, customs, and values. We hope to share with you our experiences of this great nation, which always seems to bounce back from adversity with unique, life-affirming *joie de vivre*.

Key Facts

Official Name	República Argentina	
Capital	Buenos Aires	(Short for "Puerto de Nuestra Señora Santa María del Buen Aire")
Main Cities	Buenos Aires (pop. 3 million, city only), Córdoba (pop. 1.345 million), Rosario (pop. 1.23 million), Mendoza (pop. 880,000), La Plata (pop. 724,000)	
Area	1,068,302 sq. miles (2,766,890 sq. km)	Excl. islands in the South Atlantic and a portion of the Antarctic
Geography	Argentina is located on the Southern Cone of South America.	Bordering countries: Bolivia, Paraguay, Chile (divided by the Andes mountain range), Brazil, and Uruguay
Climate	Ranging from hot subtropical in the north to cold Antarctic in the south	
Population	32.6 million	
Population Density	13.2 inhabitants per sq. km	
Language	Castellano (Castilian Spanish)	
Religion	The official religion is Catholicism.	Roman Catholic 93%, Protestant 2.5%, Judaism 2%, other 2.5% (incl. Afro-Caribbean religions mainly of Brazilian influence)
National Holidays	Independence Day, July 9; Day of the May Revolution, May 25	

Government	Argentina is a federal republic with 23 provinces and 1 autonomous city (Buenos Aires). The president is head of state. Each presidential term lasts six years. There are two chambers: the Senate (Cámara de Senadores) representing the 22 provinces and the autonomous city of Buenos Aires, and the House of Representatives (Cámara de Diputados) representing the population on a proportional representation basis.	
Currency	The peso. There are 100 cents (centavos) to the peso.	Notes: 2, 5, 10, 20, 50, and 100 pesos Coins: 1, 2, and 5 pesos and 1, 5, 10, 25, and 50 centavos
Media	The main radio stations are Radio Nacional, Radio Continental, Radio Mitre, and Radio Rivadavia available in Buenos Aires. The major newspapers are *La Nación*, *La Prensa*, and *El Clarín*.	There are five VHF channels: Channel 13 (Artear), Channel 11 (Telefe), Channel 2 (America TV), Channel 9 (Libertad), and Channel 7 (ATC), the state TV channel.
Media: English Language	The *Buenos Aires Herald*	
Electricity	220 volts, 50 Hz	Two types of plugs: 2-pronged (rounded) in older buildings; 3-pronged (flat) in newer houses. Adaptors can be purchased.
Video/TV	System PAL-N	
Internet Domain	.ar	
Telephone	The country code for Argentina is 54.	
Time	GMT -3	

chapter one

LAND & PEOPLE

GEOGRAPHICAL SNAPSHOT

Argentina is not a land of palm trees and tropical beaches, as most images of South America seem to imply. Associating a Latin American country with skiing and cold winters as well as hot and humid summers might seem odd, but this is one of many aspects that make Argentina so exciting and unforgettable.

Argentina is the eighth-largest country in the world and the second-largest in South America (after Brazil), covering a distance of almost 2,300 miles (3,700 km) from its northernmost to southernmost points. As a result, it offers an outstanding variety of scenery, climate, and geographical features.

To the west, dividing Chile and Argentina, lies the Andes mountain range, extending all the way from the northwestern corner to the southern tip of the country. The Puna is a large plain that lies at an average of 10,499 feet (3,200 meters) above sea level on the northwestern corner of Argentina near the borders with Bolivia and Chile. As you go south along the Andes you'll reach the region of Cuyo, an area whose mountains are snowcapped throughout the year. Many passes are frequently blocked by heavy

snowfalls during winter. It is in this area that you will find the 22,831-foot (6,959-meter) Mount Aconcagua, the highest peak in the Andes range, and indeed in South America.

Further south lies Patagonia, where the landscape features lakes, forests, and sharp mountain peaks near the Andes in the west, very reminiscent of an Alpine scene, and a vast semi-deserted plain as you travel east toward the Atlantic Ocean. As you approach the southernmost tip of continental Argentina, on the way to Tierra del Fuego ("Land of Fire"), named after the fires lit by the indigenous tribes of the region, you will find spectacular views of glaciers, including the world's largest, Glaciar Perito Moreno.

Nature and wildlife enthusiasts are spoiled for choice in the region of Patagonia. Whales, penguins, and many species of birds are among

the fauna of the area. Many initiatives have
been put in place to safeguard the wildlife of
the region, which, as in many other parts of the
world, is facing a rapid decline in numbers and
in some cases the sad possibility of extinction.

THE REGIONS AND CLIMATE

Due to Argentina's great coverage in terms of
latitude (a span of 34 degrees), different climates
can be observed as one travels in a north–south
direction. These range from hot subtropical in
the northwest, close to the border with Bolivia,
to freezing temperatures in the glacier regions
of the south. Visitors are advised to bring the
appropriate clothing for the regions and the
season of their visit.

The Northwest

This is a mountainous region of hot climate and
very colorful landscapes, mainly comprising the

provinces of Jujuy, Salta, La Rioja, Catamarca, Santiago del Estero, and Tucumán. It is an area of historic relics, old churches, and ruins of structures that were once part of the great Inca civilization.

The high plains of the Puna—known as the Route of the Incas—is a vast area extending well into northwest Chile, southwest Bolivia, and southern Peru. It is made up of a series of plains, 9,843 to 11,483 feet (3,000 to 3,500 meters) high, separated by lower hills mainly as a result of intense volcanic activity. It features a hot climate, with temperatures soaring during the day but dropping sharply at night.

The Eastern Andes is where the famous *quebradas* lie, a series of colorful valleys that form one of the most important tourist attractions of the area. Among them is the famous Quebrada de Humahuaca, declared a World Heritage area in 2003.

The East and Northeast

As one travels east, one finds the subtropical forests of Formosa and Chaco, rich in flora and fauna and with a hot and humid climate. This is an area of large rivers, rich landscapes, and exuberant vegetation, home to many national parks and the famous Iguazú Falls.

The rivers Paraná and Uruguay run along the eastern and western borders of the provinces of Misiones, Corrientes, and Entre Ríos. These three provinces are known as Mesopotamia, a name that in Greek means "between rivers," as does the name of the province of Entre Ríos in Spanish. Their people are cheerful, friendly, and hospitable, having developed their own style of language and music (*chamamé*) and sharing some characteristics with their Paraguayan neighbors. The work carried out by missionaries in the sixteenth and seventeenth centuries has left

behind a legacy of historic Jesuit ruins, now a
World Heritage area.

Cuyo
This region lies halfway down the country and is
comprised of the provinces of Mendoza and San
Juan, bordering Chile to the west and San Luis
to the southeast of the region. Dominated by
high peaks, snowcapped mountains, and rocky
landscapes, its climate can be quite varied due to
the influence of the Andes, with hot summers and
freezing winters as one travels west. The province
of Mendoza has gained a reputation as a producer
of excellent wines. Most grapes (of European
origin) have been grown in the region since the
sixteenth century.

The national park of Ischgualasto, or Valle de la
Luna ("Valley of the Moon"), in the province of
San Juan offers a quasi-surrealist lunarlike

landscape. This park is a paleontologist's haven, famous for its fossils, and the remains of ancient civilizations can be found here.

The Pampas

The region known as Pampa Humeda ("Humid Pampa") is the center of agricultural activity, having the richest soil in the country. It comprises the

provinces of Buenos Aires, Santa Fé, and La Pampa. It is generally flat, with two small areas of low hills in the regions of Tandil and Ventana. A temperate climate predominates, where temperatures can range from the mid-nineties Fahrenheit (mid-thirties Celsius) during the hot and humid summers (January to March) to just below the freezing point in winter.

The West and South

As one reaches Tierra del Fuego in the south, temperatures can easily reach 5°F (-15°C) in winter and climb to about 64°F (18°C) in summer. Ushuaia, its capital, is the southernmost city in the world.

To the west of the country, running along the Andes from the province of Mendoza, through Neuquén, Rio Negro, Chubut, and Santa Cruz, all the way down south to Tierra del Fuego, heavy snowfalls and subzero temperatures in winter provide the ideal conditions for winter sports. It is here that Argentina's ski resorts can be found, ranging from important international centers to smaller local ones.

THE ARGENTINIANS: A VERY MIXED BAG

Many cultures have helped to shape Argentina's society into one that differentiates itself very sharply from the rest of Latin America. British, Spanish, Italian, German, French, and most recently Korean immigrants have all found a home in Argentina. The extent to which these groups, mostly of European origin, are represented varies in number, but they make up 99 percent of the population.

On the other hand, Afro-Argentinians constitute a very small minority. Despite slavery having been no less prevalent in Argentina than in other countries until the early nineteenth century, the black community represents less than 1 percent of the overall population. The same applies to other ethnic minorities such as descendants of the original Amerindian tribes.

The Italians and Spanish

Argentina has witnessed great waves of immigrants throughout its history. The Spanish and Italians were by far the largest groups to seek new fortunes in the New World, and evidence of this is very strong in everyday life. A large proportion of surnames in Argentina are either Italian or Spanish; even local slang incorporates some Italian words. Unsurprisingly many of these communities have not developed in the same way as their European counterparts, the Italians perhaps remaining more Italian than their ancestors back home, and likewise the Spanish. This is possibly a result of being cut off from their roots and of not being exposed to those common external factors that have molded other societies over the years.

The first and second generations who arrived in Argentina still spoke their ancestors' language, and many of them spoke Spanish with a heavy accent, particularly the Galician community. As subsequent generations were born and educated in Argentina, and older generations passed away, their original languages would no longer be spoken. Typical Spanish names like Pérez, Rodríguez, and Fernández are perhaps the most common surnames in Argentina. The Italians and Spanish brought with them strong Catholic sensibilities and a firm sense of family unity that to this day remains at the heart of Argentinian values.

The English, the Scots, and the Welsh

The small British community holds an important place within Argentinian society in areas such as commerce, trade, and industry. The British in Argentina have retained a strong identity, although they have become well integrated into Argentinian society. They were instrumental in the development of Argentina's large railway network—the opportunities for employment and the skills required opened the doors to a wave of immigrants from Britain.

Left-hand Drive?
Although road traffic in Argentina drives on the right, trains still drive on the left—a legacy of British influence!

Despite a brief period of low popularity during the Falklands War in 1982, the British community continues to be represented and respected across the country. It has grown over the years, settling in many areas of the country, most of them in the capital but also in cities like La Cumbre in the province of Córdoba.

Since the early nineteenth century, Scots, Welsh, and English have arrived on the coasts of the River Plate, establishing closely knit communities and founding schools, churches, and businesses, many of which are still there to this day. Their influence is still evident in place-names such as Temperley, Wilde, and Hurlingham. Traditional private English schools are still favored by many as a paragon of good education.

Caledonian balls, bagpipes, and kilts are still very much part of life for the Scottish community, who have continued to make their mark ever since the arrival of Scottish settlers in the 1830s. These traditions have been perpetuated through the St. Andrew's community of the River Plate. Until the mid-1980s there was even a Harrods outlet in Buenos Aires, which although not officially a branch of the famous London store had the same logo and corporate branding. Today, large shops like James Smart and Wrights are flagships of British influence in Argentina.

The Welsh arrived in Patagonia in 1865 and settled in the province of Chubut, mainly driven by the search for economic prosperity. They agreed to respect the laws of the country in exchange for land and respect for their own language and customs. Welsh tea houses, music, and poetry festivals, as well as the Welsh language, are still very much part of this community.

On the sports front, rugby, golf, tennis, and polo are great icons of the British presence.

A BRIEF HISTORY

The name Argentina derives from the word *argentum*, the Latin for silver. The name was coined by the Spanish *conquistadores*, who believed in the existence of large treasures in the area they discovered upon their arrival in the early part of the sixteenth century. The River Plate is, in fact, a mistranslation of Río de la Plata, whose literal (rather than phonetic) translation is "River of Silver," *plata* being the Spanish word for the precious metal. Argentina was a Spanish colony until it gained its independence on July 9, 1816.

Early Inhabitants

Due to its vast area and marked variation in both climate and geographic features, many different Amerindians inhabited Argentina in the early days. Much of the influence of these early inhabitants

extended well beyond the borders of Argentina as we know them today. It is not surprising to see that so many centuries later, certain features and traditions are shared between those living in areas near the borders with Argentina's neighboring countries. These cultures and idiosyncrasies developed as a result of being faced with similar challenges, so commonalities can be found

between indigenous inhabitants of the Andean region of northwest Argentina stretching from the province of Córdoba all the way to the provinces of Salta and Jujuy, and their neighbors across the borders in the Bolivian, Chilean, and Peruvian Andes, where climate and landscape are very similar. Patagonia was mainly inhabited by the Yaganes and the Onas (or Patagones).

The Spanish *Conquistadores*

When the Spanish arrived on what is now Argentinian soil they found a country that was very sparsely populated. The estuary of the River Plate all the way up to Paraguay was inhabited by over fifteen different tribes, among them the Tupí-Guaraníes, Querandíes, and Mocoretás.

The regions of Chaco to the northwest of Argentina and the Pampas in the center were inhabited by tribes originally from the western part of the country near the border with Chile. Among these tribes are the Ranqueles, the Puelches, and the Pampas, who migrated eastward in search of fertile land, eventually settling in the area known as the Pampas (which includes the province of the same name). This is the main and richest agricultural part of Argentina. These tribes were the ones who, after years of contact with the Spanish *conquistadores* in the sixteenth century, developed into what are known as the *Gauchos*, later spreading to other parts of the country and adapting their ways and customs to the local environment. The *Gauchos*, however, are indigenous to the Pampas. They were nomadic herdsmen, mainly making a living by cleaning and preparing leather for the manufacture of goods. Leather was the *Gauchos'* main source of income as meat had little commercial value in those days, due to its abundant supply for such a small population, the fact that it could not be kept for long periods, and the nonexistence of any kind of export logistics. Although considered as no more than nomadic travelers in their early days, the *Gauchos* have become one of the legendary symbols of Argentinian culture and tradition, portrayed as the essence of the Argentinian character in many literary works, one of the most renowned being *Martín Fierro* by the nineteenth-century poet José Hernández.

Argentina was officially discovered in 1516 by the Spanish navigator Juan Díaz de Solís, although many writers attribute its discovery to a Florentine explorer by the name of Amerigo Vespucci (Américo Vespucio in Spanish) in 1502. Vespucci was the first to claim that the newly discovered continent was not part of Asia (as originally thought); the mapmaker Martin Waldseemuller bestowed upon him, rather than Columbus, the title of discoverer of America and so named the continent after him. Vespucci died of malaria two years before Solís arrived at the estuary of the River Plate.

The "White King"
The quest to find a passage connecting the Atlantic and Pacific Oceans dates as far back as the days of the first *conquistadores*. Solís tried unsuccessfully to find a route by sailing up the River Plate, which he had initially called Mar Dulce ("Sweet Water Sea"), but it was not until four years later, in 1520, that Fernando de Magallanes (Magellan) achieved this by venturing south down the coast of Argentina and passing through the strait that bears his name. Solís was ambushed and killed by Querandí or Guaraní Indians in 1516. Upon his death, the rest of his crew decided to return to Spain, not all of them reaching their homeland as many were shipwrecked or captured by Indians.

Among those shipwrecked was a Portuguese sailor by the name of Alejo García, who had found refuge on the island of Santa Catalina, off the coast of Brazil. Like many of his fellow sailors in the same predicament, he had heard from the Indians on the nearby Brazilian coast of the existence of a king, a sovereign of immensely rich lands to the west. According to the Indians, the abundance of gold in this kingdom was such that even the houses were built with it. This monarch, according to the locals, was not of dark skin, but more like their conquerors. Thus the legend of the "White King" was born.

Spain's thirst for conquest of the Americas continued during the reign of Charles V (Charles

I of Spain and later crowned Charles V, Holy Roman Emperor, in 1519). He sent his pilot-major, Sebastian Caboto (Cabot), to explore the River Plate; the fort of Sancti Spiritu that he founded in 1527, near modern Rosario, is considered to be the first Spanish settlement in Argentina.

The Birth of a Capital
In 1536, Pedro de Mendoza arrived at the River Plate. The purpose of his trip was threefold—to find the treasures of these new lands, to prevent Portuguese incursions into the territories, and to evangelize the native Indians. In February of that year, he founded the city of Puerto de Nuestra Señora Santa María del Buen Aire, nowadays

known as Buenos Aires. The name was given as an invocation of the Virgin Mary, a custom that had originated in Cagliari, Sardinia, which in those days belonged to Spain. Invocation of the Virgin for protection from the dangers of the sea was common practice among sailors of the Mediterranean.

The initial coexistence of the Amerindians and the *conquistadores* was a peaceful one, with the native Indians supplying food in exchange for goods. This, however, was not to last. The Amerindians became hostile and Mendoza was forced to sail up the coast of Brazil and the Paraná River in search of food. Mendoza's brother, Diego de Mendoza, remained behind, and he and those who stayed with him were attacked by over one thousand native Indians. The confrontation that ensued, the battle of Corpus Christi, resulted in the death of many Spaniards, including Diego de Mendoza.

The relative safety of the fortified city of Buenos Aires was to prove fatal. In June 1536, the city was besieged by thousands of native Indians. The Spanish were unable to obtain food and before long, starvation took its toll. One

Ulrich Schmidl, a Bavarian soldier, later wrote, "People had nothing to eat and were starving. The situation was so terrible and hunger so disastrous that rats, mice, snakes and lizards were not enough, and we eventually had to eat our own shoes and leather." Schmidl also added that there had even been cases of cannibalism among the unfortunate dwellers. The siege would eventually end when the Amerindians set the city on fire. The Spanish were forced to retreat to their ships in order to survive.

Mendoza left Buenos Aires in 1537 and died en route back to Spain. The situation in the colony remained very unstable, mainly due to the hostility of the native Indians toward the conquerors. Mendoza's successor, Domingo Martínez de Irala, decided to abandon the now besieged city and move up north to the city of Asunción (present capital of Paraguay) in search of the legendary lands of the White King.

The sixteenth century witnessed many changes on the political and religious fronts, dominated by the intense activities of the Jesuit missionaries in the province of Misiones, which was named after them. They were expelled in 1767 by Charles III of Spain for reasons that to this day are not clear. The Jesuits were, in fact, expelled from all Spanish territories, and the River Plate was no exception.

Several cities were founded toward the mid-sixteenth century, including Córdoba, now one of Argentina's major cities, Salta, Jujuy, San Luis, San Miguel de Tucumán, La Rioja, and Mendoza, the latter being famous for its wines. In 1580 Buenos Aires was founded for the second time by Juan de

Garay and became the capital of the United Provinces of the River Plate (*Provincias Unidas del Río de la Plata*).

The Journey toward Independence

By 1620 the entire River Plate region was under the administrative control of the Viceroyalty of Peru (*Virreinato del Perú*), and the colonization of the whole region in the seventeenth century began to slow in comparison to the previous century. Buenos Aires became a buoyant commercial town and by the mid-1600s its population had grown to almost 20,000.

The size of the Viceroyalty of Peru colony was too great, and it was difficult to administer and defend. The growing importance of Buenos Aires as a commercial center and the potential threat posed by expeditions by the French and British to the coast of Argentina had forced Charles III of Spain to reassess the situation in the colonies. In 1776 the territories now occupied by Argentina, Bolivia, Paraguay, and Uruguay were separated from Peru and the Viceroyalty of the River Plate (*Virreinato del Río de la Plata*) was created, with Antonio de Cevallos appointed as its first viceroy. Buenos Aires was to be the capital—this offered, among other benefits, easier access to Spain across the Atlantic.

In the late seventeenth century, Spain had started to lose its power as a great colonizing nation; at the same time, Great Britain gained power and was quickly establishing its supremacy around the world. Colonial expansion was a key factor in economic and political hegemony, which, according to the theories of the time, went hand in hand. This drove Britain to send a fleet to the River Plate under the command of Admiral Home Riggs Popham on the erroneous premise that he would find a badly defended colony, which, disgruntled with its government, would welcome the invaders with open arms. Both attempts by Britain to take control of the River Plate ended in failure with the British forces defeated by locally raised militias.

The Spanish viceroy, Rafael de Sobremonte, exacerbated an already fragile political climate by abandoning Buenos Aires, leaving the city at the mercy of its invaders. He took with him the royal coffers and sought refuge in the city of Córdoba. This not only led to Sobremonte's political ruin but also acted as a catalyst to an already growing wish for independence on the part of many settlers.

Events in Europe, particularly as a result of the Napoleonic Wars and an already discredited colonial government, provided the colonists with an opportunity to step up their fight for independence. In May 1810, representatives of Buenos Aires (the municipal council or *cabildo*) set up a provincial government that would act directly on the king's behalf, making the viceroy's role redundant. The war for independence would last for another six years; until then the country would be plunged into a series of battles between those loyal to the Spanish crown and those supporting the popular movement for independence. Among the heroes of the war for independence, General José de San Martín is probably one of the most famous. With his 5,000-strong cavalry regiment, 16,000 mules, and 1,600 horses (out of which only 511 survived), he crossed the Andes and was instrumental in gaining the independence of

Chile and Peru. This feat of Herculean proportions has made San Martín one of the most respected and venerated military heroes in Argentinian history.

On July 9, 1816, the Congress of Tucumán (*Congreso de Tucumán*) declared the independence of the United Provinces of South America (*Provincias Unidas de América del Sur*)— fourteen in total—and appointed a popular government represented by a junta, which drew up the first constitution establishing a centralized government in 1819. The ensuing years would be a period of anarchy fueled by political rivalry and the search for political stability.

Turmoil and Prosperity
Peace was restored in 1820, but the formation of a stable government remained an unresolved issue. In 1825 the neighboring empire of Brazil went to war against Argentina, as a result of disputed

sovereignty claims over the territory known as the Banda Oriental ("Eastern Strip").

In 1826 the name of United Provinces of the River Plate, adopted a year earlier, was abandoned in favor of the current name of Argentina. In 1827 the war with Brazil came to an end, and one year later the disputed territory of the Banda Oriental gained its independence, adopting its present name of Uruguay.

No sooner had peace been restored than new upheavals came to dominate the political scene, culminating in the dictatorship of Juan Manuel de Rosas. As governor of the Province of Buenos Aires from 1835 to 1852, he had managed to consolidate friendly relationships with the other provinces, thus gaining popular support. In no time he extended his authority over the rest of the provinces, quashing any opposition. It was during this period that the British occupied the Falkland Islands for the first time.

Rosas was defeated in 1852 by a group of revolutionaries headed by former governor of the Province of Entre Ríos, Justo Jose de Urquiza. The following year, a federal constitution (based on the US Constitution) was drawn up, with Urquiza becoming the first president of Argentina.

This was to be a temporary solution as Buenos Aires, refusing to abide by the new constitution, declared its independence from the rest of the provinces in 1854. In 1859 its situation became untenable, and a vanquished Buenos Aires agreed to become part of the new federation. Despite the political turmoil, it was an age of prosperity for commerce as a result of the new shipping treaties

signed with Great Britain, France, and the United States. The constitution of 1853 also declared the abolition of slavery in Argentina.

The end of the war of the Triple Alliance (Brazil, Argentina, and Uruguay) against Paraguay from 1865 to 1870 heralded a period of relative normality. In 1880, Buenos Aires was declared the federal capital of the Argentine Republic. From then on the political arena would be dominated by two groups, the radicals and the conservatives, who even to this day continue to fight for power.

From 1880 Argentina entered an era of prosperity, establishing itself as one of the richest nations in the world, aided by large waves of immigration. Agriculture, the railways, and industry in general flourished during this period. It was a time of relative peace with little or no social unrest, which would last for almost half a century.

The Right to Choose

By the beginning of the twentieth century, Argentina was one of the world's richest countries. The population had grown substantially, partly as a result of the large numbers of European immigrants who, attracted by its prosperity, had come in search of better opportunities. In 1910 Roque Sáenz Peña sanctioned the electoral law

that guaranteed a secret ballot, universal and compulsory suffrage, and the representation of all minorities.

During the First World War Argentina's neutrality strengthened its ties with the United States, both politically and economically. This continued during the presidency of Hipólito Yrigoyen of the Radical Party (Partido Radical), elected in 1916 and reelected in 1928.

After the first military coup in 1930, twentieth-century Argentina was to be dominated by military governments, with brief interludes of ephemeral civil democracy.

The Birth of Nationalism

The leaders of the military coup of 1943 had claimed as their mission the eradication of the fraud and administrative corruption that had become prevalent in the higher echelons of government. Under the presidency of General Pedro Ramírez, all political activity would be banned until the new government's aims were accomplished. Behind all this was a looming fear that the government would abandon its position of neutrality and undertake fascist activities.

Argentina's independent political standpoint during the Second World War led to the weakening of its position internationally. In 1940, President Ortiz declared Argentina's neutrality, a policy that would later be abandoned by his successors, Ramon Castillo and Pedro Ramírez. After the Japanese attack on Pearl Harbor in December 1941, Argentina and Chile were the only two American countries that refused to sever ties with the Axis powers.

This policy led to the virtual economic isolation of Argentina by the United States, which forced Argentina's government to reassess its position and to sever diplomatic relations with Japan and Germany in 1944. Fearing that Ramírez, under pressure from the United States, would declare war against Germany, a military junta forced him out of office. This new government, despite the change in foreign policy initiated by Ramírez, was accused by the United States of supporting Germany and of sympathizing with the Nazi cause. It was not until March 1945, when the Allied victory in Europe was a foregone conclusion, that Argentina declared war against Germany and Japan.

A key figure of the new regime was Juan Domingo Perón, a charismatic nationalist-populist who was to dominate Argentina's political scene for years to come. The Argentinian people had lived under military rule for too long and there was great discontent among the working class, who demanded better pay and working conditions. The presidency of Perón from 1946 to 1955 was characterized by a rise in popular movements and support for and by the working class (the Peronist or Justicialista Party). Juan and his astute wife, Eva (Evita),

portrayed themselves as defenders of the popular cause and supporters of social welfare programs and trade unions, but all at the expense of the country's economy. Argentina's people had little welfare and many of them felt they were victims of an oligarchy that was becoming increasingly powerful at their expense. Perón and Evita homed in on these feelings of discontent. When Eva died in 1952 she was greatly mourned.

Perón grew more autocratic as the economic situation deteriorated. His failed attempt to build a corporatist state and to secularize a staunchly Catholic country created a rift between the Church and government that led not only to his excommunication by the Vatican, but to the end of his administration following a coup in 1955 led by General Leonardi. Perón fled to Spain. Leonardi was later replaced by General

Aramburu, who would remain in power until 1958. Aramburu was eventually assassinated by left-wing guerillas in May 1970.

Perón made a further dent in Argentina's reputation by allowing Nazi war criminals to enter the country, where they started new lives under new identities. Among these were Josef Mengele, Walter Kutschman, Klaus Barbie, and Adolf Eichmann, who was seized by the Israeli secret service in 1960 and smuggled out of the country to stand trial in Jerusalem.

Arturo Frondizi was elected president of Argentina in the 1958 ballot. His victory was secured after Perón (now in exile in Venezuela) ordered that the banned Peronist party should support him. Frondizi's term was fraught with economic difficulties and was closely scrutinized by the armed forces, who were not keen on once again handing over power to a civilian government. Frondizi's refusal to break ties with Cuba and his handling of Argentina's domestic politics eventually led to his resignation.

There was an unsuccessful attempt by the armed forces to sabotage the 1963 elections. They feared that a victory on behalf of the Peronist movement (although banned from all political activity) would plunge the country into total chaos. Perón yet again issued orders for support to be given to two candidates who, as a result, were excluded from the electoral process. The Radical Party, headed by Arturo Illia, won the elections, but after only three years was ousted in a coup, led this time by General Juan Carlos Onganía.

For the next six years Argentina was to be ruled by military governments who continued to sow the seeds of discontent among the population. This gave rise to a series of left-wing guerrilla groups (Montoneros, FAR, ERP), many of them middle-class Catholic youths who felt they were being supported by Perón.

Confrontations between the armed forces and guerrilla groups, kidnappings, and growing violence, coupled with high inflation and strikes, forced General Alejandro Lanusse to lead the country toward a democratic solution, promising elections in 1973 in the belief that only Perón could restore order.

1,035 Days of Chaos

Hector Cámpora was to win the 1973 elections as the Peronist candidate. One month after the new president took over, and after almost twenty years in exile in Spain, Juan Domingo Perón returned to Argentina. Two million people awaited his arrival in the streets leading to the airport in an event that was marred by an armed confrontation between right- and left-wing factions of the Peronist movement, resulting in the death of 200 people. Cámpora was eventually forced to resign. After winning over 60 percent of the votes, Perón was once again, almost thirty years after he first took power, to become president of Argentina, with his new wife Maria Estela Martínez de Perón (Isabel) as vice president.

Perón's tenure was to last only a few months, until his death in July 1974. Isabel Perón took over as president, leading the country through a period rife with corruption, violence, terrorism, and political and economic chaos.

In March 1976 a military junta ousted Isabel Perón, ending 1,035 days of civilian government. Isabel Perón eventually returned to Spain, where she currently resides. The commander-in-chief of the army, General Jorge Rafael Videla, took over the presidency of Argentina, suspending all constitutional rights and political activity. This dictatorship took on as its main responsibility the eradication of all political insurgency and terrorism, mainly at the hands of the left-wing Montoneros guerrillas, and set about restoring "peace" by means of extreme repression that resulted in the death and disappearance of thousands of people.

Over 35,000 people disappeared without trial during this so-called "dirty war." One sector of society, perhaps the more affluent one, had been living in fear of left-wing terrorist kidnappings and murders, and for many this purge seemed to be a necessary evil—but it resulted in the whole population living in fear of a government that knew no bounds when it came to human rights. Both the innocent and the guilty fell prey to raids, arrests, and death.

By the early 1980s terrorism had, in fact, been eradicated. Order had been restored, but at an inhumane price, and Argentina was now led by a military government that was unpopular at best and hated at worst by the vast majority of the population. Any sense of national pride had vanished, and Argentina's image was once again tarnished.

The Falklands War and the Restoration of Democracy

One of the presidents of this period of military rule in Argentina was General Leopoldo Galtieri. Faced with political opposition, an increase in activity by the trade unions, and an unhealthy economy, Galtieri decided to occupy and reclaim the Falkland Islands in April 1982. It could be argued in retrospect that it was the defeat of Argentina by Britain in this conflict that sealed the fate of military rule in Argentina.

Sovereignty over the Falklands had been an issue for more than a century. Claims of sovereignty had been made by both Britain and Argentina, and although the matter had never been resolved there had been a peaceful coexistence, with the Kelpers (the inhabitants of the Falklands) using Argentinian mainland facilities and regular weekly flights to and from the mainland. The junta's original intention had been to enter into an armed conflict with Chile over a stretch of land in the Beagle Strait. This never happened—the fact that the Chileans were only next door and were well armed probably served as a good deterrent.

Britain, on the other hand, was far away. Argentina launched an attack on the assumption that Britain, being so distant and probably unconcerned about two small islands in the South Atlantic, would not retaliate. This proved to be a costly mistake.

On March 31, 1982, the people of Buenos Aires took to Plaza de Mayo to demonstrate against Galtieri and the government, only to be met with fierce repression from the police and the army. Two days later, on April 2, they congregated with great euphoria to hail Galtieri as a hero for the invasion of the Falklands.

The government thought that it had achieved the patriotic unity so long desired and that this would help to clear Argentina's name after years of repression. Argentinians of all sectors of society, including many people radically opposed to the government, agreed that the Falklands should be Argentinian. This was a false sense of patriotism driven by a purely external factor. Support for this cause had become the norm, and those not in favor were branded as pro-British and enemies of the country.

By June, Argentina had suffered a terrible defeat at the hands of the British. Many young conscripts had been sent to fight against one of the best-trained professional armies in the world. Argentinian pride had been hurt like never before; even though foreign reports on the progress of the war had been banned, the outcome was clear weeks before the end of the conflict. Again people took to the streets, but the mood was very different from that of April 2.

Faced with total loss of credibility, low morale, inflation of over 200 percent, poor salaries, and now a discredited armed forces, Galtieri was replaced by General Reynaldo Bignone, who vowed to be the last military president of Argentina. Bignone legalized political activity. In 1983, Raúl Alfonsín won the elections as head of the Radical Party, whose government eventually brought to trial the members of the past juntas, including those responsible for the invasion of the Falkland Islands, charging them with human rights abuses. Argentina's economy was still ailing and would not recover for a few years to come.

Carlos Menem of the Peronist Party won the elections in 1989 and again in 1995. This was the first time in over half a century that power in Argentina was handed from one elected government to another. Menem's first presidency was characterized by a period of political stability and prosperity driven by a program of liberal economic policies in the hands of his minister of economy, Domingo Cavallo. It was during this period that a one-to-one parity with the US dollar was established.

However, corruption and administrative fraud slowly led the country to the brink of economic collapse. Menem's successor, Fernando de la Rúa of the Radical Party, found the national coffers virtually empty. Massive unemployment and hunger among the population led to the ransacking and looting of food outlets. This forced de la Rúa to take extreme and painful measures. Prompted by a run on the banks, he issued a decree limiting the withdrawal of funds to 1,000 pesos per month.

Sadly, the damage had already been done as over one billion dollars had already been taken out of the country. In an unprecedented series of events, the population took to the streets banging pots and pans and were met by harsh repression at the hands of the authorities. De la Rúa finally bowed to popular demand and resigned, leaving behind a crippled economy and a national industry in a state of decay.

De la Rúa's successor, Néstor Kirchner, faced the daunting task of getting the economy back on its feet, and the year 2004–05 witnessed a slow yet realistic improvement. Argentina had bounced back time and again from economic and political adversity. However, any sustainable economic recovery was to be short-lived. In 2007 Cristina Fernández de Kirchner took over the presidency from her husband after winning over 54 percent of the votes in the general elections. Argentina once again entered a period of sluggish growth and growing inflation.

Following President Kirchner's unsuccessful attempt to amend the constitution to allow her to run for a third term, Argentina went to the polls in 2015 amid a return to social, economic, and political uncertainty and a weak opposition who, to date, seem to lack the unity to present a credible alternative.

GOVERNMENT AND POLITICS

Argentina is a federal republic divided into twenty-three provinces and Buenos Aires, the federal capital. Its constitution was modeled on that of the United States, and as in many similar republics the executive power is held by the president, alongside the legislative and judicial powers. The constitution is still that which was drawn up in 1853, although it has been subject to subsequent revisions. The latest of these, in 1994, enables the president to be reelected and extends the term of office from four to six years.

Legislative power lies in the hands of the Congress, made up of the House of Representatives (Cámara de Diputados), representing the population, and the Senate (Cámara de Senadores), representing the twenty-three provinces and the federal capital.

For the last sixty years the political arena has been dominated by two major parties, the Radical Party (Partido Radical) and the Justicialista Party, the legacy of the old Peronist Party, currently in power.

THE ECONOMY

Argentina is a country with a huge wealth of natural resources, including oil, gas, and minerals. With over 30 million hectares of arable land yielding over 60 million tons of cereals and oleaginous crops, it

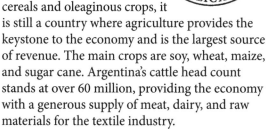

is still a country where agriculture provides the keystone to the economy and is the largest source of revenue. The main crops are soy, wheat, maize, and sugar cane. Argentina's cattle head count stands at over 60 million, providing the economy with a generous supply of meat, dairy, and raw materials for the textile industry.

Industry has made rapid gains in Argentina; of these, food, beverages, and tobacco account for one-third of the country's output. Textiles, rubber, and leather represent one-quarter of the country's industrial production, with chemical industries

and oil refineries accounting for another quarter.
Other industries are transportation, machinery,
and manufacturing, the latter being heavily
dependent on imported raw materials.

However, over the last few years the economy
has suffered and output has fallen as a result of
the government's economic policies, including

non-payment of creditors and investment funds. Argentina's seemingly uncompromising position has affected the government's credibility, and it has been faced with potential sanctions from the IMF as a result of unreliable economic data.

MAJOR CITIES
Buenos Aires

The capital and largest city in Argentina, with a population of just under 12 million, including the federal capital and greater Buenos Aires, accounts for one-third of the population of Argentina. The capital itself has a population of 2.7 million. Built along the banks of the River Plate, it is the main entrance into Argentina, a dynamic and vibrant city of imposing architecture, broad tree-lined avenues, theaters, cinemas, galleries, cafés, and a magnificent opera house. Buenos Aires has been deservedly called the Paris of South America. The wide range of architectural styles—from old Hispanic colonial buildings to magnificent neoclassical palaces and modern glass and steel designs—places Buenos Aires in a league of its own. Its sophisticatation is reminiscent of Paris or Madrid, yet it preserves a strong element of local tradition in its music (tango), its language (with its distinctive accent), and its vociferous and friendly people (the *Porteños*).

Like many large cities, Buenos Aires is a fast-moving place. It is the seat of the government and of many international corporations. In 1978, despite controversy about the politics of the military government, Argentina hosted the

football World Cup, with Buenos Aires as the focal point for the event. This had a deep impact on the infrastructure of the city and its attitude to visitors. Argentina's victory helped to unite he country and briefly created an atmosphere of joy and celebration. Argentinians are still passionate about the sport and the rivalry between the two main teams, River Plate and Boca Juniors, continues to dominate the football scene in Buenos Aires and, indeed, across the country.

Buenos Aires has a lot to offer, from its elegant shopping streets to food of epicurean standards. Plaza de Mayo, San Telmo, La Boca and Palermo, and the stylish area of La Recoleta, show different facets of the city and should not be missed. From a cultural perspective, the Museo de Bellas Artes (Fine Arts Museum) holds regular exhibitions of international caliber, and the Palacio Errázuriz houses the museum of decorative arts.

Music lovers will be able to choose from a wide range of genres, from the local music (tango) shows to excellent jazz at the traditional Café Tortoni. The Opera House is one of the finest in the world, featuring a roster of international artists during its opera and concert season in a magnificent auditorium with first-rate acoustics.

Between 1880 and 1920 the face of Buenos Aires changed profoundly. Urban growth and changes in technology were accompanied by social and cultural transformation as a result of the numbers of immigrants from Europe that arrived in Argentina. More than 3.3 million people entered the country between 1857 and 1914. These people brought with them cultures, values, and norms that have played a key role in Argentinian society right up to the present day.

The *Porteños* are stylish and sophisticated and extremely fashion conscious. Their mannerisms, accent, customs, and roots are diverse and set them apart from the rest of the population.

Córdoba

Located in the center of the country, Córdoba is the second-largest city in Argentina with a population of just under 1.5 million. Córdoba has always been an important political, economic, and cultural focal point. Its founding was driven by the desire to link the River Plate with Peru. The tribe of Indians known as Comechingones created some of the greatest pictorial relics in Argentina here, having left over 1,000 paintings and etchings in many caves.

Córdoba is a city of great heritage in terms of its architecture and historic relics. Its university, founded in 1613, is the oldest in Latin America. It is popularly known as the "city of bells," a nickname inspired by the large number of churches built by the missionaries. It is a city that offers a wide range of museums and green spaces such as the Parque Sarmiento, which dates back to the late 1800s.

Córdoba was host to important political events in the twentieth century and has continued to be a focal point for union activities. Notable examples are the student revolt of 1918, when students took to the streets to demand educational reforms, and the event known as "*El Cordobazo*" in May 1969. The latter, led by the government of the then President Juan Carlos Onganía, resulted in the death of fourteen people when students and workers clashed with police and armed forces while demanding the end of a ban on union activities.

Córdoba's role as a center of industrialization began in 1927 with the opening of a military aircraft factory, and was consolidated thirty years later with the opening of large automobile and textile factories. The *Cordobeses* are friendly and determined, yet very different from their more provincial neighbors. They possess a very distinctive accent, extending the length of their vowels in an almost musical manner.

chapter two

VALUES & ATTITUDES

FAMILY FIRST

Argentina, like most Latin American and
Mediterranean nations, is a country of strong
family values. Despite changes in social norms,
the family remains a solid institution. It is normal
even today for children to live with their parents
until they get married, although the more
European custom of leaving home after reaching
a certain age is increasing. The main determining
factor is a financial one, as property is expensive
and until a few years ago mortgages were not
commonplace; even now, when mortgages are
available, not many can afford them.

City dwellers lead a life not dissimilar to
that of the inhabitants of any big city, and the
difference between life in Buenos Aires and
the quieter rural life of the remote areas of the
country could not be greater.

Family gatherings (particularly on Sundays)
are the norm; usually this extends to uncles, aunts,
grandparents, and cousins, so these events can
become very lively. Children come first and are
welcome in most places. They are looked after,
brought up, and educated to the parents' best ability
and constantly encouraged to compete and succeed.
In turn, it is common for the younger generation to

look after their elderly parents; in many cases, parents move in with their children. There is a constant quest to maintain this family unity. It is still common practice for children to go to university near their home when possible; children require written authorization to travel abroad with only one parent, and parental approval for many things is

sought, although not necessary. It is these strong family ties that have helped many survive harsh economic climates and political instability.

For Argentina, the last thirty years or so, since the reestablishment of democratic government in 1983, has been a period characterized by a feeling of having to make up for lost time. The last two decades have brought about many changes. Fewer people get married, opting instead simply to live together. The number of single mothers has risen, perhaps as a result of an increased ability on the part of women to gain financial independence and escape conflictive or violent marriages.

La Gauchada

This is a term used to refer to a special favor. It represents an attitude, a friendly way to request help when asking someone to do something outside their normal duties.

WOMEN

As in many Mediterranean cultures, where men have traditionally been the breadwinners and women have largely been responsible for running the house and looking after the children, the deep-rooted concept of *machismo* is evident in Argentina. This is stronger in more provincial and rural communities, as the role of women in Argentina's society has changed dramatically in recent years; women are now influential in the fields of politics, business, the arts, and science.

In the early 1970s, a series of feminist movements began to establish a change in the role of women in Argentina. Their work and emancipation was hindered by the arrival of the dictatorship in 1976, but their presence was still visible. Since then women have become key players in the day-to-day development of Argentina's society. The ousting of president Fernando de la Rúa was, in fact, initiated by women—they took to the streets *en masse* banging their pots in protest, a tactic that proved

much more effective than the use of armed force.

The *Madres de Plaza de Mayo* have made their cause heard all over the world. They exerted pressure on the government to release details of the whereabouts of their missing children, who were among the thousands who disappeared at the hands of the military government.

In Argentina, 55 percent of students across all levels are women, although women account for 51 percent of the population and one-third of Argentina's workforce. This is leading to a higher number of qualified women. As a result of this, the biggest rise in female employment has been in the fields of science and technology, with an increasing number of non-qualified women being unemployed. To this day, salary differentials between men and women who perform the same task and corporate glass ceilings for women persist, although these are slowly giving way to an egalitarian approach, perhaps influenced by foreign companies who take a very different view of what is due to working women. The assertive behavior and tenacity of women continue to act as strong catalysts for ongoing change.

PROUD TO BE ARGENTINIAN
Argentinians have been defined as Italians who speak Spanish, think they are Britons living in Paris, and like to earn American salaries.

National pride extends to many, but not all, areas—food, clothes, way of life, and, of course, football. Areas such as politics and the economy are not something Argentinians tend to boast about. Patriotism as a value has not really existed in Argentina until recently. Unstable economic situations and a general mistrust of incompetent governments have made people adopt a justifiably selfish attitude, putting themselves first, irrespective of whether it is good for the country or not.

Argentinians tend to be forgiving and fair. The jingoism that was inculcated in them during the military dictatorship, and that led to great animosity between Britain and Argentina during the Falklands War has, fortunately, not survived. However, governments tend to use the issue of sovereignty over the Falklands as a red herring in an attempt to distract people's attention from more domestic issues. Patriotism and national pride come as the norm rather than as a value, mainly when driven by external events such as

an armed conflict or an international sporting event. When Argentina hosted the World Cup in 1978, and won it, people took to the streets in celebration, even as others were quietly disappearing in the so-called "dirty war."

DISCIPLINE AND HONESTY

Discipline is not a national trait yet. Argentinians are not in denial when it comes to recognizing this. From driving to trying to beat the system, their behavior is certainly not as orderly as a visitor might expect. Given the option of bending the rules slightly to their own advantage, they will take it. If confronted with their actions, they will admit fault but shrug. Argentinians are basically honest people who for many years have been in the hands of dishonest governments, high taxation, and crippling laws. This has resulted in a very cynical approach to life, particularly to politics and the system as a whole, and people often try to find a way to cut corners.

Who you know is still more important than what you know. *Palanca* (leverage) is still very much in use when it comes to looking for a position within an organization, both in the public and private sectors. Knowing the right person will in many cases count more than skills and competencies, although this is admittedly more prevalent in the public sector. The private sector prides itself on being professional and adequately staffed when it comes to skills and qualifications. Argentinian professionals spend up to six years at university, combining their studies with full-time work in most cases. Discipline may not be their strength, but they are hard-working and tenacious.

Bribery (*coima*), a result of poor pay among civil servants and an inefficient bureaucratic apparatus, is widespread in certain sectors. Policemen, traffic wardens, and civil servants have been known to accept bribes. It is wise not to engage in such practices; if faced with a potential problem with the authorities it is best to contact your embassy or consulate.

Loopholes in the system will be exploited with a self-gratifying sense of having outsmarted the rest. This attitude (*viveza* or *piolada*) has given the Argentinians a bad reputation among other Latin American countries, who see them as supercilious and arrogant.

COMMUNITY AND INDIVIDUALISM

Argentinians are very sociable but do not have a strong community spirit, outside that generated by the church they might attend. Working as a team or in a group is therefore quite hard for them, as each member will probably try (albeit not maliciously) to outsmart the rest, and hidden agendas will almost certainly play a part. The education system is not designed to produce team players, but stars. This is evident in politics, business, and even the arts, where merit is ascribed normally to one individual rather than to a group of people.

Argentinians are generally individualists, and teamwork is not the norm. Perhaps due partly to a permanent mistrust of their political leaders, people have developed an attitude of putting themselves first at the expense of collective effort. Collective accomplishments are not usually recognized, and Argentinians will tend to single out an individual to give credit to for an achievement—or to point the finger of blame at, should things go wrong.

This does not mean that all Argentinians are indifferent to their community or their country. There are groups of people, notably the younger generation, who are developing a stronger sense of community. Protecting their environment and their national heritage, and a sense of responsibility for looking after their own country, are values that are slowly being embraced by a new generation. Nevertheless, graffiti and the defacement of public property are still very much in evidence, although the authorities are trying to clean this up and help Buenos Aires maintain its well-kept character.

Argentina's younger generation is the first to have been born and raised under a democratic system. It is essentially more liberated than previous generations, and so exposed to the same malaises as its peers in historically more democratic societies. Some values seem to have been either eroded at best or to have broken down at worst. Over the last decade in particular there has been a visible trend toward lack of discipline in schools and less respect for teachers and authority as a whole. The sort of behavior associated with the authoritarian regimes of the past seems to have given way to a somewhat misplaced sense of entitlement.

THE CHURCH AND RELIGION

Argentina is a staunchly Catholic country where abortion is prohibited and divorce was not merely frowned upon but illegal until 1987. There is a strong correlation between Argentina's culture and religion, which reinforces a philosophy predicated on the belief that there is an absolute "Truth"— the Argentinian attitude tends to be "There can only be one Truth, and we have it." Other religions are represented but are no more than minorities within the 93 percent Roman Catholic population.

The role of the Church in Argentinian society is still very important. Through the ups and downs of political and economic upheaval, the Church seemed to provide solace, and in many cases food and shelter. Argentinians can be pious, but not to the extent found in other Catholic countries. With the arrival of democracy, people have become much more open in the expression of their feelings and opinions. Attitudes to sexuality have changed, and the Argentinians have embraced liberal views on sexual matters that would be considered reprehensible by those adhering to strictly Catholic values.

A large proportion of the population are

devout believers. Attending Sunday mass is commonplace, and although more people have looked for comfort in religion during troubled times, the Argentinians have always been quite observant of the Catholic values that were brought by their Italian and Spanish forefathers.

Names also reflect Argentina's staunchly Catholic heritage, particularly the use of the names of Mary and Joseph. Traditionally female names like María are frequently used as second names for men, and by the same token the traditionally male name José can be used as a woman's middle name. María José is a woman's name, while José María is a man's name.

The pilgrimage from Buenos Aires to Luján is perhaps the largest of its kind. The fifty-mile walk takes place every October, with over 1 million devout Argentinian Catholics taking part. During the Falklands conflict in 1982, Pope John Paul II became the first pope to celebrate mass in the Basilica of Luján. However, this event has probably been overshadowed by the nomination of the Argentinian Cardinal Jorge Bergoglio as Pope Francis. Despite the elation and pride in most Argentinians' hearts, the relationship with the Kirchners (both Cristina and her late husband) has been tense and far from amicable at times. In 2014 Cristina Fernández de Kirchner attempted to smooth the relationship, although many claim this move was for political gain rather than a genuine attempt to mend bridges.

Luján: A Touch of Divinity

Luján holds a special place within the Catholic faith in Argentina. It dates back to 1630, when the Spanish, *en route* to Santiago del Estero in the north of the country, found themselves unable to move a cart carrying a statue of the Virgin Mary. This was taken as a sign of the Virgin's wish to remain in that place. A sanctuary was erected that would house the statue until 1730, when the first church was built. In 1887 the foundation stone of the wonderful Gothic-style Basilica of Luján was laid. In 1930, 300 years after the arrival of the Virgin, Luján was declared patron city of Argentina, Uruguay, and Paraguay.

WORK ETHIC

The Argentinian business community has been compared with royalty who, though temporarily down at the heels, fully expect to regain their rightful place in the world. Argentinians are, by and large, hardworking individuals who until recently were not accustomed to a very competitive environment. The arrival of technology, the globalization of the economy, and the resulting quest for cutting costs and maximizing profits, particularly during adverse economic periods, have created a culture of aggressive marketing tactics and more diverse working practices.

Multinational organizations have brought with them new approaches and a more meritocratic work ethic. The older generation has found this hard to come to terms with, being from a very hierarchical society where length of service weighs more heavily than achievement when it comes to seniority within an organization. This new work ethic is slowly superseding the old Argentinian way of doing things, whereby everything needed to be adapted to the Argentinian way rather than the Argentinians adapting to new ideas.

Argentinian society generally has a low level of tolerance for uncertainty. In an effort to minimize or reduce uncertainty, strict rules, laws, policies, and regulations are adopted and implemented with varying degrees of success. Individual Argentinians have a tendency to control everything in order to eliminate or avoid uncertainty. As a result, they will rarely embrace or even accept change and will tend to be very averse to risk taking.

chapter three

FESTIVALS
& CUSTOMS

PUBLIC HOLIDAYS

There are eight fixed public holidays in Argentina.

New Year's Day January 1	
Good Friday March/April	
Labor Day May 1	
Anniversary of the First National Government (known as "Day of the May Revolution") May 25	
Independence Day July 9	
Discovery of America Day (*Día de la Raza*) October 12	
Day of the Immaculate Conception December 8	
Christmas Day December 25	

There are three movable public holidays. These move to the previous Monday if they fall on a Tuesday or Wednesday, or to the following Monday if they fall on a Thursday or Friday.

Veterans Day and Day of the Fallen in the Falklands War April 2
Flag Day (Death of General Belgrano) June 20
Anniversary of the death of General Jose de San Martín August 17

THE IMPORTANCE OF FOLKLORE

Argentinian folklore is based upon the music and customs of the countryside rather than on myths and national stories. The customs and traditions of the early Spanish settlers blended with those of the later European arrivals to give rise to a uniquely Argentinian folk culture. This features traditional forms of clothing such as the poncho, weapons such as *boleadoras*, horse saddles and riding styles, and food and drink. Many of these folk elements have become potent symbols in Argentinian literature, painting, and music, and their importance continues to be upheld although practices have changed over the years.

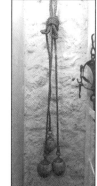

Folklore therefore occupies a special place in Argentinian culture. There are many days in the calendar that, while not always official public holidays, are celebrated with parades, *asados* (barbecues), pageants, or musical and cultural events. These are some of the more noteworthy.

Day of the National Anthem May 18

Day of the American Indian April 19

Day of the National Flower (the ceibo) November 22

Day of the Gaucho December 6

Tradition Day (honoring the birth of José Hernández, the author of *Martín Fierro*) November 10

National Flag Day (paying homage to the flag's creator, Manuel Belgrano, on the day of his death) June 20

Boleadoras

These consist of three balls made of stone, wood, or nowadays metal, covered in leather and each attached to a length of rope. A legacy of the early Indian tribes who used weighted thongs as a hunting weapon (with only one ball until the eighteenth century), these have become a symbol of *Gaucho* culture.

Two variants of the *boleadoras* can be found. Used as a weapon for combat, they developed into their current form of two balls of approximately the same dimension and weight that are flung around in order to gain momentum, plus a smaller ball which is held in one's hand until the weapon is thrown. For hunting purposes, the *boleadoras* consist of two spheres only and are thrown at the prey's legs, wrapping themselves around and causing the animal to trip over. These were mainly used to hunt *ñandú*, a local variety of the ostrich.

The *Ombú*

Despite its huge size of 49 to 66 feet (15 to 20 meters) high, the *ombú* is categorized as a herb due to its hollow trunk, which can grow up to 15 feet (4.5 meters) in diameter. It can be found mainly in the eastern part of the country, in the provinces of Corrientes, Entre Ríos, Buenos Aires, and Santa Fé. Isolated in the middle of the vast countryside, its rich foliage and large trunk provide shelter from the rain, the sun, and the wind. Its leaves are also used for medicinal purposes. It cannot be used for carpentry or industrial purposes or even as firewood due to the hollowness of its trunk.

The *Facón*

The *facón* is a large dagger used as a weapon as well as a utensil. The word is a derivative of *faca* (old Spanish and Portuguese for "knife"), to which the augmentative suffix *on* has been added to convey the meaning of "large." The *facón* consists of a pointed blade about 12 inches (30 centimeters) in length that slides into a sheath originally made of leather, which was usually clipped or attached to the *Gaucho*'s belt. Nowadays they are also sold as ornaments made of silver or steel.

Truco

This actually translates literally as "trick." It is a card game mainly played in the region of the River Plate (Buenos Aires and Santa Fé, extending to neighboring Uruguay). Played with a pack of forty "Spanish Cards" (*cartas españolas*) as opposed to standard playing cards, it is a fast-moving team game enhanced by a series of gestures that players use to tell each other the cards they hold without tipping off their opponents. It is normally played by two or three groups of two players, with teams inviting each other to accept certain challenges based on the cards in hand. As these are accepted the players start laying their cards on the table, the winning team being the one holding the cards with the highest value combined with the highest number of points, given according to the challenges accepted or declined. While visitors can master the basic rules of *truco*, learning how to play it goes well beyond this; the art remains a great local skill that outsiders will find very hard to master.

MATE: MORE THAN AN INFUSION

Mate (loosely pronounced "mah-tay") is the traditional Argentinian hot drink. The *mate* drinking custom is widespread in Argentina, and although *mate* is an acquired taste, it is something all visitors must try at least once.

The word *mate* refers to both the container and the herb (*Ilex paraguensis*, known as *yerba mate* to differentiate it) that is actually infused. The preparation may sound simple, but there is a hidden art to making *mate* (*cebar un mate*), and a badly prepared offering could be an insult to the

connoisseur. The *yerba mate* is infused in boiling water in the container (*mate*) and drunk with a sophisticated straw called a *bombilla*. The *bombilla* is normally made of stainless steel, although cane and silver ones can also be found. *Mate* is taken without sugar in most cases (*mate amargo*). It can be a very social drink, and passing one *mate* around a group can be common among drinkers. When drinking it, care must be taken not to block the *bombilla* with the *yerba mate*.

Yerba mate was one of the many new things the Spanish *conquistadores* came across upon their arrival, together with potatoes, tomatoes, and wheat. *Mate* had initially been banned by the Jesuits, who claimed that the herbs were the cause of the indolence and lethargy of the locals and thus would bring about their own ruin. It was considered a vice, and those breaking the rule would face excommunication.

Mate is now more than an infusion, it is a symbol of the land. Ornamental *mates* can be purchased both for use and as ornaments.

NATIONAL CELEBRATIONS

There are countless feasts, festivals, and traditions across the country representative of the cultural backgrounds of the various Indian tribes who inhabited the land for centuries. One example is the Quechua festival of *Inti Raymi* ("Festival of the Sun"), celebrated every year in the city of Salta on June 20, the day of the winter solstice.

There are religious celebrations and festivities such as the pilgrimage to Luján (see page 61 above) as well as a series of originally pagan celebrations such as *Carnaval* in the month of

February. Food and harvest festivals are widespread and vary according to the region and the time of year. Due to the importance of agriculture, many regional festivals are more important for the rural population than for city dwellers, many of whom may not even be aware of their existence.

Many festivals, in particular wine and food festivals, are the direct result of European

influence, as opposed to traditional Amerindian festivals, which consist mainly of harvest celebrations or other religious rituals. A typical Argentinian *fiesta gaucha* (*Gaucho festival*) consists of various events such as rodeos (*doma de potro*) where one can witness horsemanship skills at their best, folk music and dancing, and of course a lavish Argentinian barbecue.

Christmas and Epiphany

The main Christian holidays are strictly observed, Easter and Christmas in particular. Unlike Anglo-Saxon cultures, Christmas Eve rather than Christmas Day holds greater importance. The traditional family occasion consists of dinner on Christmas Eve, when presents are given, with more observant families attending midnight mass.

Many people celebrate Epiphany (*Reyes Magos* or simply *Reyes*) on January 6. Children receive presents on this day (rather than on Christmas Eve).

Easter and Holy Week
Easter (*Pascua*) and Holy Week (*Semana Santa*) play an important part in the Catholic Argentinian calendar, with masses celebrated across the country.

The period of Lent is known as *Cuaresma* (that is, a period of forty days), and Palm Sunday is known as *Domingo de Ramos*. Buenos Aires receives thousands of visitors during the Easter period, many of them attending the main Catholic celebrations in Luján and Buenos Aires Cathedral.

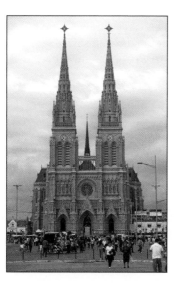

chapter four

MAKING FRIENDS

FRIENDS AND ACQUAINTANCES

Meeting people, making friends, and socializing
are as easy in Argentina as in most Latin cultures.
Visitors are welcomed with open arms and the
Argentinians will show their hospitality in every
possible way. Argentinians tend to make friends
easily. Many long-lasting friendships date back to
early school days. People may fall out with each
other, but the Argentinians tend to take friendship
seriously and will be quite forgiving.

Socializing is a very important aspect of life
for the Argentinians, who will rarely miss an
opportunity to go out and meet people. Although

their close friends tend to be few in number, Argentinians will have many acquaintances. It is normal for groups of friends to get together in each other's homes or go out for meals.

Inviting visitors home is customary, and one will be made to feel part of the host's circle of friends and acquaintances. Argentinians love to entertain, and they prefer to do so in their own homes, or their weekend homes (*quintas*) should they have them. Barbecues (*asados*), coffee evenings, and having guests over for dinner and parties are all characteristic of Argentinian hospitality. Repeated invitations will signal one's acceptance into the circle of friends.

An invitation to Sunday lunch, in many cases a barbecue, is a great occasion to meet people over a meal that can start at noon and still continue four hours later.

Talking is a great Argentinian pastime, be it at home with family or over a coffee outside the

home. The Argentinians are well-educated people who are happy to converse for hours on end about politics, sports, current affairs, or their favorite hobbies. They have no inhibitions and are very direct when expressing their views about politics, but one should not give one's opinion unless asked. Some topics are to be avoided. These include the Falklands War, a subject that many people are still sensitive about, and Juan Perón (or his wife Eva), as one will soon find that Perón was either venerated or hated. Care should be taken when making comparisons with other Latin American countries, particularly regarding the rivalry between Argentina and Brazil (remember that in Brazil, they speak Portuguese).

GESTURES AND PHYSICAL CONTACT

Physical contact in Argentian culture is about the same as in other Latin societies. Handshaking between men and women as well as among women is customary in a business context. When meeting someone socially, a degree of informality prevails— kissing someone of the opposite sex on the cheek (only once) is the norm.

When it comes to proxemics (the rules of personal space), Argentinians tend to stand closer to each other than the northern Anglo-Saxons. This could cause discomfort to some visitors, who may feel that their personal space is being invaded. In the countryside, the rules vary slightly, with people standing a trifle further away from each other. Intense eye contact should be avoided as it could be construed as challenging or aggressive. Avoiding eye contact, particularly outside the realm of the larger cities, should not be interpreted as a sign of insincerity; intermittent eye contact is probably the best approach.

Body language is used a lot; touching, hand gestures, and facial expressions always help to convey the speaker's message and enhance the listener's interpretation.

SOME DOS AND DONT'S

Gestures to be avoided include many one would avoid in most other Western cultures.

- The "thumb and forefinger circle" gesture stands for OK—unlike in neighboring Brazil, where it is vulgar and offensive. The "thumbs up" gesture can be used freely as it also stands for OK.

- Brushing one's chin with the top of one's hand outward means "I don't know."

- Beckoning people to come, particularly if accompanied by a "psst" (as some Brazilians tend to do), is rude—Argentinians will normally extend their arm with their hand palm facing down and make a "scratching" motion with the four fingers to beckon someone over.

- Yawning in public is considered rude and is best avoided.

TIMEKEEPING

Timekeeping is mainly determined by context and in more informal social occasions is almost irrelevant. Start times for concerts, plays, and similar events are normally observed, although a ten-minute delay is not uncommon.

When it comes to parties, lunch appointments with friends, barbecues, and similar nonbusiness-related events, start times are only indicative. If invited to a party it is not advisable to arrive on time—in fact, your punctuality might even be considered rude. If arrangements have been made to be picked up from your hotel or home, a good degree of flexibility should be observed; waiting by the door ready to go at the prearranged time could result in a long wait. Arriving on time at parties is simply not trendy!

Being kept waiting is normal, and if the other party should arrive late at a restaurant or a meeting and display little or no compunction this should not be taken as a sign of lack of respect or consideration. The polychronic Argentinians will probably be juggling with several things at once.

Early dinners (as in Anglo-Saxon cultures) are not the norm, particularly if one is eating out. In popular restaurants it might even be hard to find a table as late as 11:00 p.m.

SOCIAL DRINKING

The drinking of wine is an important part of social activity. Wine is drunk with ordinary meals and it is not unusual for parents to give watered-down wine to their children, particularly at barbecues and Sunday family meals. Argentinians drink well, sensibly, and with discernment. Public drunkenness is rare, frowned upon, and not considered a necessary part of having fun. Less sophisticated drinkers will mix wine with soda, particularly less expensive wine.

The province of Mendoza on the slopes of the Andean foothills is the center of wine production in Argentina. The long, sunny days, high altitude, and wide temperature ranges provide the necessary ingredients for the making of high-quality wines. Immigrants from Italy, Spain, and France have left their mark on Argentina's wine industry, leading to the planting of a wide range of grapes in the region of Cuyo, with Lujan de Cuyo being renowned for its full-bodied reds and its own appellation. Toward the northwest of the country, the vineyards of Cafayate in the province of Salta are home to a variety of Torrontes, an excellent aromatic dry white wine.

Chardonnay and Pinot Noir are the result of high-altitude vineyards and are among the finest

Argentinian wines. Malbec was for many years the most popular red grape, having yielded Malbec wines in some cases far superior to their French counterparts. Malbec has given way to other grapes such as Bonarda. From Cabernet Sauvignon to Zinfandel and Nebbiolo, there is no shortage of choice. Caro 2000 by Domaines Barons de Rothschild and Nicolas Catena is a wine that has made its mark; it has a strong Argentinian identity, heralded by Malbec, blended with Cabernet Sauvignon. The combination has made a rich and refined wine, a harmonious balance between the Argentinian and Bordeaux styles.

Alcohol is freely available around the clock in bars, and there are no licensing restrictions of any kind other than on the sale of alcohol to minors. Unfortunately, beer drinking has become more common among young people, often accompanied by displays of unruly

behavior. Binge drinking is seen as an extremely antisocial habit; Argentinians are very self-conscious when it comes to maintaining their dignity, and inebriation is considered extremely unbecoming. Going to a bar before a party or social event and turning up drunk will be an irreparable mistake. All the same, the freedom that democracy has brought with it has resulted in an alarming increase in the consumption of alcohol, particularly among adolescents and young adults and particularly among the lower-income bracket of Argentinian society.

While many cultures get together "for a drink," in Argentina having a coffee (*tomar un café*) is still the norm. This is an activity that takes place in the many pavement bars and cafés of Argentina, from the exclusive La Biela in the elegant district of Recoleta in Buenos Aires to more modest ones all over the country.

GIFT GIVING

Gifts do not necessarily need to be solid objects. Sometimes a favor in exchange for another is more appropriate and more welcome than a tangible gift (see pages 143–4).

In social contexts it is impolite to arrive at someone's house empty-handed. Chocolate, flowers, or a bottle of (good) wine are appropriate gifts. Bringing something for the hosts' children is always a nice touch, and it need not be anything expensive. For more celebratory occasions like weddings and christenings, Argentinians tend to be very generous when it comes to gift giving. Wedding registries (lists) are the norm, and one should try to give a gift from the registry. Money should not be given as a gift as this practice is reserved for immediate family.

If traveling to a foreign country it is a nice touch to ask one's friends or colleagues if there is anything they need from that country, as imported goods are heavily taxed and sometimes hard to obtain.

CLUBS AND SOCIETIES

Clubs, with very few exceptions (such as the very exclusive Jockey Club), are relatively easy to join. There are many clubs and gyms where different sports can be practiced. Membership fees vary according to location, size, and facilities.

For the less athletic visitor there are literary societies, book clubs, and theater groups that carry out their activities in English. The *Buenos*

Aires Herald (see page 156) lists a calendar of weekly activities with contact telephone numbers in many cases. Theater groups such as the Suburban Players, who have been staging plays in English for over forty years, are good entry points for English speakers to mix with expats and Anglo-Argentines without having to worry about the language barrier. The American school (Lincoln School) in Buenos Aires and the Asociacion Argentina de Cultura Inglesa have a calendar of activities and events that offer good opportunities for meeting people.

Musical activities such as choral societies are excellent places to meet people and obtain a taste of Argentina's cultural life too. Although the language barrier might prove to be a slight hindrance, one is very likely to find one or two English speakers.

chapter five

DAILY LIFE

STANDARDS OF LIVING

Both quality of life and standards of living have changed over the last thirty-five years, and more dramatically over the last decade. For many years Argentina's society differentiated itself from the rest of Latin America by having a predominant middle-class majority, with minorities of very affluent and very poor people. Most people enjoyed, with varying degrees of affluence, a relatively good quality of life, and hunger and abject poverty were almost nonexistent.

The socioeconomic changes sparked by political instability and corruption in the 1980s

and 1990s have affected the quality of life and standard of living of Argentinians across the whole spectrum of society. There are still very wealthy people, and Argentina's middle class continues to spend money but at a slower rate. Prosperity and comfort have given way to poverty, hunger, and soaring unemployment, resulting in an increase in violent crime.

There are more enclosed private neighborhoods (called *countries*), and people have become more security conscious than ever before, even though crime rates and threats to personal safety are not as serious as in other Latin American countries.

The number of people living below the poverty line has risen sharply as a lingering result of hyperinflation and of unsound economic policies and austerity plans. People who cannot afford a roof over their heads tend to live in shantytowns (*villa miseria*), which, once confined to the outskirts of the city, have been spreading across more inner-city areas.

For Richer, for Poorer

The Argentinian middle class likes to live well and to appear to be doing so. Restaurants are always full, nightlife is very busy, and, despite straitened economic circumstances, people continue to dress and look much as they would in more prosperous times. It can be baffling to many visitors that aside from street beggars, picket lines, and political demonstrations, life, particularly in large cities, seems to be business as usual.

Welfare provision has increased dramatically under Cristina Fernández de Kirchner's presidency. This has been criticized as political manipulation by those who view it as encouraging many to adopt living on state hand-outs as an alternative lifestyle. On the other hand, the number of people below the poverty line is expected to reach unprecedented levels; the government's own figures are extremely conservative, if not deliberately misleading.

Despite the non-too-healthy state of the economy, many Argentinians continue to travel abroad, despite currency exchange restrictions and crippling surcharges on payments made abroad using credit cards (which in 2014 stood at an additional 35 percent).

SCHOOLS AND EDUCATION

Argentina has a very high literacy rate, with almost 97 percent able to read and write. There are ten years of compulsory school education starting from the age of five. Free state education is provided across the country, although there are also many private schools around, many of them providing the curricula of the International Baccalaureate or British GCSEs and A-levels. These schools tend to be expensive and can only be afforded by a minority.

The academic year runs from March to November with a break in July (winter holidays) and a long summer break. State school pupils (both boys and girls) do not wear uniforms but a white pinafore called a *guardapolvo*. Teachers wear it too. The Argentinian education system has undergone many changes since the end of the last dictatorship, when the curriculum was biased in terms of content in areas such as history and current affairs, and debate and questioning were not encouraged.

Despite these changes and a move toward a more Socratic approach to education (as opposed, in this case, to autocratic), there is room for improvement and there are still critics of the system who claim that it is inadequate and substandard. As it is, Argentina still produces excellent professionals, scientists, doctors, and artists, including two Nobel laureates.

When it comes to university education there are again private and state universities. Those wishing to attend university must sit for a common entrance examination (*exámen de ingreso*). State universities and higher education institutes charge nominal fees, while private establishments are more costly. University lectures are normally structured in shifts, allowing students to work (even full-time) while studying. Many universities offer late evening timetables from 7:00 to 11:00 p.m. Sadly, underfunding and strikes by teachers and administrative staff as a result of economic instability have affected university education quite severely.

NATIONAL SERVICE

Following an incident that led to the death of an eighteen-year-old soldier, which brought to light the way young conscripts were being mistreated in a number of garrisons across the country, compulsory national service was abolished in Argentina in 1994 during the government of Carlos Menem. This was replaced by a voluntary national service scheme whereby volunteers receive remuneration in exchange for their services for up to ten years. There have been talks of a return to a compulsory format for those who neither work nor study, but this remains a controversial issue and no firm decision has been made to date.

HOUSING

The choice of where to live is very much conditioned by the state of the economy, and it is almost impossible for younger people to buy their own property. The more affluent live in large houses in the suburbs or very large apartments in the elegant areas of the city center. Buenos Aires has no shortage of properties to rent, and most young people who move away from home will tend to rent an apartment. These can vary in size and price according to the area in which they are located.

Finding a Place to Live

In the main cities finding accommodation is relatively easy, be it apartments to rent or residence inns for shorter stays. There are many real estate agents, although visitors are well advised to deal with them through an interpreter or else find an English-speaking agent who will look into such details as rates, expenses, and any unresolved legal matters, and contact the building's managing agents.

Due to the prices of property in relation to Argentinian income, there are many people who live in rented accommodation. The city center is, as in most countries, where most people live. However, there are options in the suburbs of Argentina's largest cities that are worth considering. Once again, the *Buenos Aires Herald* lists real estate agents as well as properties for rent. Harold Hyland, J. Reynolds, and Manson are some of the real estate agencies that employ English-speaking staff.

TOWN AND COUNTRY

Argentina is a predominantly agricultural country, and the symbiosis between town and country is

perpetuated through the established families of landowners who to this day still earn much of their income from the land but live prosperously in the city. This interdependence becomes evident in events such as the *Exposición Rural*, which takes place annually in July/August in Buenos Aires. This great exhibition, which has been going on year after year for well over a century, offers buyers, breeders, producers, and the general public the opportunity to see Argentina's best of breed under one roof, from show jumping to cattle shows and prizes for best of breed animals. There are also stands promoting the latest agricultural machinery, new hybrid crops, cattle food, and the most recent developments in nutrition and veterinary research.

DAILY ROUTINE

Daily life in Argentina is hectic—particularly in Buenos Aires, where people work long hours. In many households where both parents work, children are often looked after by relatives until one of the parents returns home. Most children who attend state school attend for half a day, while those attending private schools tend to study both morning and afternoon.

Shopping, looking after the children, and running a house are carefully balanced to ensure that the children are given the required attention. Modern facilities such as supermarkets offering late shopping have become necessary ingredients of daily life.

The Working Week
Office hours in Argentina are perhaps slightly longer than elsewhere—from 9:00 a.m. to 7:00 p.m., Monday to Friday. The extended lunch break, normally lasting between one and a half to two hours from 12:00 p.m. to around 2:00 p.m., may account for the later finishing hour. In the main cities shops are normally open Monday to Friday from 9:00 a.m. to 8:00 p.m., and on Saturdays from 9:00 a.m.to 1:00 p.m. Shopping

centers are generally open seven days a week from 10:00 a.m. to 9:00 p.m. (and in some cases as late as 11:00 p.m.).

The *Siesta*

Although still a regular habit in provincial towns and rural communities, the rest period after lunch known as *siesta* is no longer common in Buenos Aires and other large cities. Perhaps a lingering vestige of the *siesta* break continues to be the extended lunch break, although fast food and sandwiches seem to have become as prevalent as big sit-down meals, perhaps driven by a combination of a younger generation and budgetary constraints. In the interior of the country, the *siesta* is a practice still observed, particularly in areas of very hot weather where temperatures can be too high for outdoor work at midday.

USUAL WORKING HOURS AND OPENING TIMES

Banks and Bureaux de Change Monday to Friday 10:00 a.m. to 3:00 p.m.

Office Hours Monday to Friday 9:00 a.m. to 7:00 p.m., lunch break from 12:00 p.m. to 2:00 p.m.

Post Offices Monday to Friday 8:00 a.m. to 6:00 p.m., Saturday 8:00 a.m. to 1:00 p.m.

Shops Monday to Friday 9:00 a.m. to 8:00 p.m., Saturday 9:30 a.m. to 1:00 p.m.

Shopping Centers Monday to Sunday 10:00 a.m. to 10:00 p.m.

THE COST OF LIVING

Despite the more favorable exchange rates and the peso being one of the most depreciated currencies in the world, Argentina is not as inexpensive as it used to be. This is symptomatic of the current economic instability, inflation, and government policies. Many prices are set at US dollar values and are therefore on a par with international prices. However, it is possible to find a range of prices to suit different budgets.

For a large part of the population who earn in pesos, however, life is a struggle. Argentinians as a whole have become very price conscious and have become more parsimonious in their spending habits. The upper middle class still earns relatively good salaries, and it is they who keep the restaurants full and can afford vacations abroad.

The precise inflation figures are a topic of some controversy. The official figures are well below what is reflected in the increase in prices. These are massaged by the government, to the opprobrium of both Argentinians and foreign opinion, but estimates are that inflation hovers around 20 to 25 percent. It is ironic that one of the richest countries in the world, the breadbasket of Europe during the Second World War, could, as a result of mismanagement and corruption, reach a state of such economic instability.

FAMILY OCCASIONS

There are important milestones in Argentinian family life. Some of these are in line with Catholic tradition. Baptism, first communion, and weddings are perhaps the three most important events in Argentinian religious life.

Baptisms have changed over the last few years, having become a generally much more intimate occasion celebrated in the company of immediate family and perhaps a few friends, although this may vary from family to family. Presents are given and usually consist of silverware, picture frames, books, Christian images, or earrings for girls (normally gold or pearl).

First communion can be preceded by several months of religious education (catechism). The church ceremony is followed by a luncheon attended by close family and friends, although nowadays there is a tendency for those who can afford it to mark the occasion with a big celebration. Girls normally wear a white dress and boys wear what is probably their first suit.

Weddings are perhaps the biggest event; ceremonies in the church are normally followed by receptions, ranging from small family gatherings to lavish banquets and huge parties. The bride will wear a white dress and the groom a suit or other formal attire. By and large, Argentinian weddings are no different from those in many European countries. Registry ceremonies take place a few days before the church wedding.

Secular Celebrations

A girl's fifteenth birthday is a very important event that is traditionally celebrated with a big party (or *quinceañero*), either at home or in a hotel or similar venue. The girl will usually wear a dress purchased or made specially for the occasion. Traditionally she will have the first dance (usually a waltz) with her father, who will then invite his daughter's partner and the rest of the guests to take to the dance floor. Nowadays new ideas are often introduced, and the arrangements and entertainments at one event may differ from those at another.

The traditional cake ceremony is worth a mention. The white-frosted cake is attractively decorated with ribbons. Just before it is cut, the young girls present gather round, and each takes hold of a ribbon. All together, they pull their ribbons from the cake, and each finds a small charm attached to the end of her ribbon, usually of silver. One of these will be a horseshoe or a ring, to bring good fortune to the lucky recipient.

As with many traditions, things are changing with the times. These days girls often want something different, and perhaps expect more excitement than is offered by an old-fashioned party with cakes, ribbons, and waltzing with their father and uncles. Today, travel agencies offer special packages for fifteen-year-old girls (or the "rose" market, as it is locally known), and the number choosing a trip, abroad or within the country, seems to be growing apace.

Graduation from school may be celebrated with a class excursion. The destination will vary according to the families' means, with the city of Bariloche remaining a favorite.

chapter six

TIME OUT

Argentinians know how to have a good time. Their idea of leisure can vary from a lazy afternoon to a day of sporting activities. Barbecues and entertaining at home are popular; the weather is a great contributor to outdoor leisure activities and men and women will tend to spend quite a bit of their leisure time in the sun.

From football matches in public parks to water sports and yachting for the more affluent, Buenos Aires and the center of the country with its more

temperate climate provide the ideal conditions for outdoor activities almost all year-round.

RESTAURANTS AND COFFEEHOUSES

The café culture that can be seen in cities like Paris or Madrid is very present in Argentinian everyday life. It is still customary for people to get together for a coffee in one of the many *confiterías* (tea houses, loosely translated) that can be found in most large cities (see Social Drinking, page 76 above).

When it comes to restaurants, Argentinians are spoiled for choice. Going out for a meal is still very much a social event where conversation can continue over coffee long after the meal is over.

Food and Drink

Argentina is renowned for its excellent quality of food, catering to everyone from the gourmet to the more functional eater. Compared to many Latin American cuisines, Argentinian food is not normally spicy, and is perhaps not as exotic.

The most typical Argentinian food, and perhaps the one that has gained the best reputation, is beef. *Parrillada* (mixed grill) or *asado* consisting of barbecued steak as well as various other parts of the animal such as sweetbread, kidneys, and black pudding are very much part of Argentinian gastronomic culture. *Chorizo*, a mildly spicy sausage barbecued and served hot, is still the most common appetizer

served at barbecues, not to be confused with the Spanish *chorizo*, which is served cold and is more akin to salami. *Empanadas* are small pastries usually filled with meat, chicken, or sweet corn (*humita*); these again

are served as a first course or appetizer.

The influence of the great waves of immigration from Spain and Italy, mainly the latter, can be seen in some aspects of Argentinian cuisine. Argentinian pizza, which according to experts is among the best in the world, has retained its traditional recipe throughout the decades.

International cuisine has also made its mark in Argentina. French, Japanese, Chinese, Thai, Basque, Greek, Hungarian, and Arab restaurants can be found alongside outlets selling other Latin American cuisines such as Mexican and Chilean. Also present are the ubiquitous fast-food chains, which can be found in main shopping centers and busier districts.

For Those with a Sweet Tooth
Whether in the afternoon or in the morning, *facturas* are a must. These are delicious pastries that come in various shapes with different fillings such as custard, cream, and jam. *Media lunas* (croissants, literally translated as "half moons")

are perhaps the most common form of *facturas*, usually accompanied by a cup of coffee, tea, or hot chocolate. It is interesting to note that *factura* is also the Spanish for "invoice"!

What's for dessert? For those wishing to delve into truly Argentinian desserts, *dulce de leche* is a good place to start. Literally translated as "milk jam," it is akin to toffee but softer and lighter. Made from condensed milk that is boiled until it acquires a brown color and toffeelike consistency, it is used as a spread or as a filler for pastries and pancakes. Crème caramel (*flan*) topped with a dollop of *dulce de leche* is a popular choice.

A local alternative to the ubiquitous Mars bar, KitKat, or the like is the *alfajor*. This is a small round cake usually covered in chocolate and filled with *dulce de leche*.

TIPPING

Tipping is more common in Buenos Aires than elsewhere, although the practice seems to be slowly becoming prevalent across the country. In restaurants it is customary to leave a tip of 10 percent of the total bill. Some restaurants will include a service charge of up to 25 percent, in which case a minimum tip should suffice.

It is also normal practice to tip hairdressers, ushers in cinemas and theaters, and taxi drivers, the latter usually by rounding up the fare. Tips are not generally expected, so you are unlikely to be confronted should you fail to leave one.

TABLE MANNERS

Table manners in a social and business context are broadly the same.

- Blowing one's nose at the table is not done.
- The use of cutlery is the same as in continental Europe, and the use of toothpicks should be avoided despite their presence on many restaurant tables.
- Both hands should be kept on the table. The custom of eating with one hand on one's lap should be avoided.
- When one has finished one's meal, one should place the cutlery side by side across the plate.
- As in most Spanish-speaking countries, the word used for a toast is *Salud!* (literally, "health"). Incidentally, this is also said to a person who has just sneezed.

Smoking

Smoking is not considered as antisocial a habit as it has come to be regarded in Western Europe or the States. Despite the usual health warnings, smoking is still widespread, with over 40 percent of the adult population succumbing to the habit. Antismoking awareness campaigns have stepped up their efforts with limited success, although since 1994 there have been nonsmoking areas in restaurants and bars.

Smoking in shops, cinemas, theaters, and public transportation, however, is forbidden, as it is in some public offices, and the ubiquitous *prohibido fumar*" notice is a visible sign of the times.

If sitting at a table, asking others if it is all right to smoke is still the norm, so lighting up just after a meal with little regard for others is not advisable.

SHOPPING

Shopping in Argentina, especially in Buenos Aires, can be quite an experience. Stylish and fashionable shops abound, with many local designers alongside the renowned international labels.

Clothes, footwear, leather goods, books, and antiques are only some of the things that are on offer across a huge number of retail outlets. There are many shopping centers across Buenos Aires, most of them offering a plethora of outlets to meet all budgets, from the stylish Patio Bullrich in the city center to large American-style shopping malls in the suburbs with shops, food outlets, and cinemas. These are also convenient as they have longer opening hours than usual, normally from 10:00 a.m. to 10:00 p.m., including Sundays.

Buenos Aires has many shopping districts, from the stylish, elegant, and quite pricey Recoleta to more modestly priced retailers like those found on Avenida Santa Fé. Florida, a pedestrian street since 1913, is still an important retail area stretching over 1,094 yards (1 kilometer) from the elegant San Martín Square (Plaza San Martín) to Avenida de Mayo, where a variety of shops, cafés, and arcades can be found. It is still a shopping landmark of the city center of Buenos Aires.

Round-the-clock shopping is not usual; where available, it is restricted to the main cities and is limited to newsdealers and selected shops. In smaller cities and provincial towns, lunch breaks can be quite long and it is not uncommon to find shops closed between 1:00 p.m. and 4:00 p.m. Sunday trading is also limited to larger cities, with varying opening times. Gas stations usually open early in the morning and close at midnight.

Kioskos

Kioskos are very much part of the character of Argentina's towns and cities. Unlike newsdealers in the UK, *kioskos* normally sell confectionery, cigarettes, and soft drinks. These are usually small shops, with a few being no more than a counter or shop window, and the customer being served on the sidewalk. Normally found in stations and busy streets or near bus stops, the *kioskero* will always readily help in giving directions or information about buses.

Duty-Free Shopping

In line with most taxes in Argentina, value-added tax (VAT) is quite high at 21 percent. If buying goods in Argentina, one can reclaim the VAT (IVA, *impuesto al valor agregado*) on items over a certain value (US $70 at the time of writing). It is important to point out that only single transactions of this value or over will qualify for a VAT refund. This means that two separate purchases of US $35 will not qualify, but one single purchase of US $70 will. It is worth bearing this in mind when you come to plan your shopping.

As in most countries, VAT can be reclaimed on purchases made in outlets that are registered with the VAT office. These display the traditional "tax free" logo in the window. It is worth asking before purchasing, particularly if the purchase in question is of high value, as the tax refund can be quite considerable.

Visitors should give themselves enough time when going to the airport in order to complete the formalities of a VAT refund. One must obtain the relevant forms from the retailer, and upon completion of the formalities at customs the reimbursement will be made in cash, a debit to one's credit card, a personal check, or a money order payable to the customer in any branch of Global Refund around the world.

Banks and Cash Machines

Banks and cash machines are found in most places in main cities. Care should be taken when withdrawing cash from machines on account of an increase in muggings. There are various retail banks, many of them branches of international main street banks such as HSBC, Citibank, and BNP Paribas.

There are also many currency exchange offices (*casas de cambio*) where money can be changed. It is best to check the rate of exchange and the amount of commission payable first. US dollars are easier to exchange than pounds sterling, although euros are also accepted by most banks and bureaux de change. Like in many other countries there is a parallel (or gray) market offering a much more favorable exchange rate for foreign currencies, particularly the US dollar (known as *el dolar blue* to distinguish this from the official exchange rate). Changing money in the street will provide a better exchange rate (almost twice the official rate). However, this is against the law and can pose a risk to personal safety, and potential prosecution, and is thus best avoided.

THEATER AND CINEMA

The Argentinians are great cinema and theater lovers. Cinema buffs will find that Argentina has more to offer when it comes to choice of films than many other places. The blockbuster American films are shown alongside French and Spanish films, productions from other countries, and, of course, Argentinian films, many of which have won the acclaim of international audiences

and critics. Films in Argentina are subtitled and not dubbed except on very rare occasions.

Buenos Aires boasts over one hundred cinemas and ninety theaters, which makes it the city with the most intensive theatrical activity in Latin America. Although productions are in Spanish there are a few amateur and semiprofessional groups that stage productions in English, notably composed of members of the Anglo-Argentine community. Groups such as the Suburban Players have been staging high-quality plays and musicals for more than fifty years. They offer a good way for visitors to get involved with the local community without the language barrier, by either acting or performing more administrative tasks.

The cultural centers of Borges Recoleta and General San Martín are hubs of national and international cultural activities, featuring concerts, recitals, plays, exhibitions, and lectures.

NIGHTLIFE

There is no shortage of nightlife in Argentina's main cities and holiday resorts during peak periods. Bars and restaurants are open until the early hours of the morning, and finding a table in a popular restaurant even as late as midnight can be a problem.

Buenos Aires nightlife is probably among the most active in the world. The more affluent *Porteños* will kick off the evening with a meal, which will rarely start before 10:00 p.m. Clubs and discos open fashionably late—you should arrive no earlier than 1:00 a.m.

Fashion consciousness is at its peak in some of the most exclusive bars in Buenos Aires, where dress is smart yet informal. Palermo, Las Cañitas, Puerto Madero, and Recoleta are at the center of nightlife, with many bars, restaurants, and clubs accounting for busy streets all night long. Tango bars and shows, jazz cafés, and live music venues are mainly found in the city

center, with many bars serving food too. Cinemas have late night performances and many theaters offer two evening performances on weekends.

Argentina (and Buenos Aires in particular) is still a favorite destination of many international pop groups including The Rolling Stones, Pink Floyd, Paul McCartney, Deep Purple, Coldplay, Britney Spears, Shakira, and many others. Venues for such events are football stadiums (River Plate being one of the largest and most popular) and the Luna Park, an indoor arena in the city center of Buenos Aires.

Sex and the City

As in any other large city, strip bars and adult entertainment are openly advertised in Argentinian cities, as well as "services for men and women" as seen in the national press. Sexually transmitted diseases are as much of a risk here as in many other countries. Visitors should avoid the notoriously disreputable areas of the city.

LOTTERY AND GAMBLING

Gambling laws have been relaxed since the arrival of the democratic process in Argentina. Casinos now operate in most provinces, offering the usual range of games such as blackjack, roulette, baccarat, and slot machines. The casino in Buenos Aires is located in the busy nightlife district of Puerto Madero on a Mississippi-style boat. Casinos can also be found in most popular seaside resorts, such as Mar del Plata and Pinamar. Casinos are the most prevalent form of gambling in Argentina.

The lottery (*Lotería Nacional*) has a series of gambling products such as *La Grande*, the largest lottery prize draw in Argentina, which has been in existence since the late nineteenth century. Bingo, *quiniela* (a type of lottery), and lotto are also available. *El Gordo de Navidad* is the big lottery draw at Christmastime. The draw is broadcast on the radio, and the winning numbers are "sung" by children as they are drawn. This Christmas draw has been taking place for over a century, with the top prize reaching 1.8 million pesos (about US $585,600/ £320,000).

Football pools in Argentina are called *PRODE*, an abbreviation of *pronosticós deportivos* (literally translated as "sports forecast"). There are thirteen matches, whose results must be correctly guessed in order to win. Prizes are awarded for thirteen, twelve, or eleven correct results for football matches played on Saturdays or Sundays.

Horse racing is of course very popular, representing the fourth-most popular form of gambling after casinos, *quiniela*, and bingo.

SUMMER PLACES
The choice of summer resorts varies according to taste and budget. The seaside resorts of the Atlantic coast are by far the most popular as they are within easy reach of the main cities of

Buenos Aires, Córdoba, and Rosario, and there is plenty of accommodation to suit all budgets. Places like Mar del Plata and Pinamar (about 250 miles from Buenos Aires) attract many visitors during January and February.

The hills of Córdoba are also a popular destination for those who seek a vacation away from the crowds and prefer hiking, cycling, and fishing. There are plenty of hostels and hotels as well as a wide range of properties to rent.

The landscapes and natural beauty of the winter ski resorts in the south of the country attract visitors from all over the world in summer too. Lakes, mountains, and the great outdoors are the choice of many families, both with and without children, in these areas where summers are not as hot as in the rest of the country.

One of the most exclusive summer resorts continues to be the seaside resort of Punta del Este across the River Plate in neighboring Uruguay. This is where the affluent Argentinians

spend their summer vacation along with visitors from many other countries; even the former Shah of Iran used to have a house here. This is a place that thrives on tourism, with beaches, all-night clubs, restaurants, yachting, and properties that are on a par with many Beverly Hills mansions. For the younger generation, Punta del Este is *the* place to be seen, and although many people consider it a "poser's paradise" akin to many Californian resorts, it is still the chosen destination for many well-to-do Argentinians.

Some people own a holiday home in Argentina, often in the south or in the most popular seaside resorts. Those who own farms or *estancias* will opt to spend all or part of their vacation there.

Open Spaces
Whether in a small rural town or a large city, squares (*plazas*) are always found. Large cities tend to have many squares and green spaces. Palermo is a vast area of Buenos Aires with

several parks, surrounded by an elegant residential area. There are many attractions in these gardens, including the planetarium, a boating lake, the botanical gardens, and the zoological gardens. Palermo also has smaller enclosed gardens such as a Japanese-style garden, a rose garden, and a patio built in Andalusian style.

Other main cities have no shortage of green spaces, such as Parque Sarmiento in Córdoba and Parque San Martín in Mendoza, which also houses the zoo.

HIGH CULTURE

The European roots of Argentinian society are reflected in much of its music, literature, and lifestyle. Concerts, recitals, and ballet, although found in main cities only, are of very high quality. No visitor should leave Buenos Aires without visiting the magnificent Opera House (Teatro Colón), one of the best of its kind in the world

and with acoustics that are second to none. Its sumptuous auditorium, which has been host to the world's top orchestras and artists for almost a century, also houses the Buenos Aires Philharmonic Orchestra.

The Italian and German influence in Argentina laid the foundation for a great operatic tradition. The opera season at the Teatro Colón features many of the works in the standard repertoire alongside lesser-known pieces. There are over two hundred performances at the Teatro Colón every year, one hundred of which are operas, sixty-five are concerts, and thirty-five are ballet performances.

For those interested in music and singing, there are many choral societies that visitors can join. These will provide the enthusiast with the chance to get involved in local cultural life and to sing under the baton of some of the world's great conductors.

An Underground Art Center?

The Teatro Colón was originally located in Plaza de Mayo in the building that now houses the Central Bank. The need for a larger auditorium prompted the construction of the current building. It occupies about 86,000 square feet (8,000 square meters), of which 54,000 square feet (5,000 sq. m) belong to the building itself, while an astonishing 32,000 square feet (3,000 sq. m) lie below Arturo Toscanini Street, housing all the workshops, wardrobes, rehearsal halls, and catering facilities, and the Music Academy (Instituto Superior de Arte).

The visual arts and literature also offer an interesting combination of European cultural heritage and local culture. The National Fine Arts Museum (*Museo Nacional de Bellas Artes*), Museum of Modern Art (*Museo de Arte Moderno*), Museum of Hispano-American Art (*Museo de Arte Hispanoamericano*), and Museum of Decorative Arts (*Museo de Arte Decorativo*), all in Buenos Aires, have a varied program of exhibitions and lectures. Museums are open five days a week, normally Tuesday to Saturday and in some cases Wednesday to Sunday; it is advisable to check before going. Most museums are closed on Mondays.

Argentina has produced many celebrated artists across many disciplines: Jorge Luis Borges, Ernesto Sábato, and Julio Cortázar in literature; Raul Soldi, Quinquela Martín, and Antonio Berni in painting; and Martha Argerich, Daniel Barenboim, and Lalo Schifrin in music.

As in many countries, cultural life in Argentina revolves around the capital city. Despite the cultural centralization of Buenos Aires, where most museums and art galleries can be found and where most cultural events take place, archaeology, natural sciences, and natural history museums can be found in other cities around the country.

POPULAR CULTURE
Tango
It would be difficult and unfair to ascribe a single popular culture to Argentina—you'll encounter many as you travel across the country. Many areas

have their own music and traditions. Perhaps the most widespread is the popular *Porteña* culture, in view of the fact that 33 percent of the population live in Buenos Aires.

Tango is perhaps one of the most famous popular music styles in the world. Tango, however, is not a national dance. It is found mainly in Buenos Aires, with other parts of the

country having their own dance forms. Tango originated as a dance among the impoverished classes of Buenos Aires, characteristic of bordellos and places of ill repute. It eventually developed into music that was to captivate the whole spectrum of society, yet retain its inherent underlying tones of melancholia and desperation. The arrival on the scene of great exponents of the genre like Carlos Gardel transformed the perception of tango, thus giving it a coveted place in the popular culture of Buenos Aires. Tango is a genre that can be found in its purely instrumental or sung forms. Lyrics reflect the sadness and joy of *Porteña* life and its characters, and are characterized by melancholy and sorrow.

Tango continues to flourish as a musical style and has transcended the boundaries of Buenos Aires popular culture through the work of artists such as Astor Piazzolla. There has been a rise in the popularity of tango among the younger generation over the last couple of decades. Many schools have their own dedicated tango dance groups and even their own tango orchestras. There has been a large increase in the number of places where one can learn how to dance tango; this is an excellent way of taking in the local culture, as are the many venues where tango is performed.

The district of La Boca in Buenos Aires remains the place that embodies the spirit of tango. Certain parts can be rather touristy, but it still retains a character that makes it worth spending a few hours in.

Folk Music

There are several styles within Argentinian folk music, perhaps musically not as sophisticated as tango, which developed much under European influence. It is in the folk traditions that the influence of the indigenous native peoples who inhabited Argentina at the time of colonization becomes evident.

There are several musical forms, including *baguala*, which originated in the tribes of more advanced cultures such as the Diaguitas and Calchaquíes. These forms originated in the area of the province of Tucumán and spread to the high plains of the Andes. This is music still strongly built upon a five-note (pentatonic) scale that can vary from slow and gentle to quite vivacious in the high plains of Salta and Jujuy. *Yaraví* originated in the Inca culture of Peru and made its way to the northern part of Argentina. It expresses pain and sorrow.

These old musical forms have given way to today's musical styles, such as *zamba*, *gato*, *chacarera*, and *chamamé*. Most of these are played on a guitar accompanied by percussion (normally a drum, or *bombo*), and in the case of *chamamé*, indigenous to the area of Mesopotamia, an accordion will also feature.

Carnavalito is a style very characteristic of the region of the Puna up in the Andes that shares a lot in character with the music of Bolivia and Peru. Typical of this genre is the use of many regional instruments, such as the *quena* (similar to a recorder), the *siku* (also known as the "pan

flute"), and the *charango*, a stringed instrument whose sound box is made from the carcass of an armadillo (*mulita*) with a wooden lid covering it and a fingerboard attached. Originally fitted with gut strings, modern versions are made of wood and fitted with metal or nylon strings. The style of *carnavalito* and its typical instruments was used by Simon and Garfunkel in their 1970 hit "If I Could" (also known as "*El Condor Pasa*").

SPORTS

There is no shortage of sporting activities in Argentina, and facilities for most of them are quite good. A wide range of sports is played, with football being the most popular. The infrastructure for professional football is very good, with some stadiums seating over 40,000 people. Although the last World Cup held there was almost thirty years ago, the stadiums built for the event are still in very good shape. For the football enthusiast, the traditional River Plate versus Boca Juniors match is perhaps the single most important football game in the first division.

The British influence again makes its mark when it comes to rugby, tennis, and golf. Los Pumas, Argentina's national rugby team, are almost always present at international rugby tournaments. There are several rugby clubs one can join, offering opportunities to players of most ages and abilities. The Buenos Aires Lawn Tennis Club hosts international tournaments featuring many of the world's top-seeded players and offers pretty well-structured courses and coaching.

Again, there are several clubs one can join, many of them dedicated tennis clubs.

Argentina's climate is ideal for golfing. Fertile land and a temperate climate provide the conditions for excellent turf and all-year-round playing. Golf came to Argentina with the British in 1879 when a Scotsman, Henry Smith, arrived with the first set of golf clubs. The Argentinian Golf Association organizes a series of national and international tournaments.

The Golfing Craze

There are more golf links in Argentina than in the rest of Latin America combined. The Argentinian Golf Association lists 243 affiliated courses, with twenty-seven of them par three, and administers the handicap of almost 45,000 players nationwide!

Polo is a sport dominated by the more affluent sectors of society. Argentinian polo is renowned for the high standard of its players and the best of breed horses used. Many international figures, including HRH Prince Charles, have at one time or another played polo in Argentina. *Pato* is the popular form of polo; it was declared the national sport in 1953. It is played on horseback, and the ball (the *pato*) is caged inside leather straps with handles so that the players can seize it and pass it to each other. The object of the game is to score points by putting the *pato* through a

metal hoop. It is a fast-paced sport that requires a fair amount of bravado.

Along Argentina's coast, particularly in the province of Buenos Aires, a large number of enthusiasts take to the water in their crafts. Sailing, waterskiing, rafting, and motorboating can be practiced all year-round. There are several yacht clubs within easy reach of the city center, and particularly the suburbs to the north of the center, offering excellent and convenient mooring facilities.

The resorts in the south of the country offer the opportunity to practice winter sports in well-equipped centers with very good infrastructure for skiing and snowboarding. For the more adventurous and experienced enthusiast, mountain climbing in the Andes offers challenges equal to many of the world's large mountain ranges. Hang gliding and rafting have been gaining popularity over the years, aided by the country's spectacular scenery and geography.

chapter seven

TRAVEL, HEALTH, & SECURITY

WHEN TO GO

It is worth remembering that the seasons in the southern hemisphere are the opposite of those in the northern hemisphere. The high season in Argentina is January and February, when schools break for the summer vacation. There are also winter school vacations in July. As Argentinians escape to their favorite resorts by the seaside, in the south of the country, or in the hills of Córdoba, accommodation and transportation can be harder to find. Advance booking is recommended during these busy periods.

Buenos Aires can be visited all year-round, although December, January, and February can be very hot and humid. Days are long during these summer months, making this the ideal time of year to visit Patagonia, where temperatures are more bearable than during the cold and blustery winters. Conversely, the soaring temperatures in the north and northwest do not make this region the best destination in summer. During winter (June to August) temperatures are more bearable, although they can drop sharply after sunset. For those seeking to admire the subtropical vegetation

and natural beauty of the Iguazú Falls, winter and spring are the best times to visit as the weather is cooler and there is less rain.

The winter months offer the ski enthusiast the opportunity to take to the slopes in one of the many resorts in the Andean region of the country. Needless to say, adequate clothing is required for the sub-zero temperatures.

ENTERING ARGENTINA
A valid passport is required to enter Argentina. Nationals of some countries will also require a visa; it is best to check with the Argentinian consulate if this is the case. Visitors arriving from non-neighboring countries are allowed to bring in up to US $300 in goods without paying any import duty or local taxes and an additional US $300 in goods acquired in local duty-free shops. This is correct at the time of print but visitors are advised to check in order to avoid additional charges.

Visitors will normally be given permission to remain up to ninety days as a tourist. If you envisage a longer stay, it is best to check with the consulate before departure as to what should be done to avoid unnecessary delays and being caught up in the Argentinian bureaucratic apparatus when trying to regularize your stay in the country. Outstaying your permitted period is not recommended.

Vaccination certificates are not required except for cholera and yellow fever for visitors from areas where these diseases are endemic. Argentina possesses a very high standard of inoculation campaigns, and the vast majority of the population is inoculated against polio, smallpox (now eradicated), and tuberculosis.

Plants, fruits and vegetables, and perishable foods are not allowed into Argentina. Pets are allowed provided adequate proof of vaccination can be shown.

TRAINS

Despite the once great train network that boasted over 24,856 miles (40,000 kilometers) of railways, trains are used for suburban to city-center commuting but are no longer commonly used for long-distance journeys. Sadly, this once enviable network has fallen victim to neglect and lack of investment. Long-distance trains are not very comfortable, serve few destinations, and services are not frequent. Journeys can take many hours, and for those who can afford it, flying has become the preferred means of long-distance travel.

There are four terminal railway stations in Buenos Aires where frequent and reliable services to the suburbs depart and arrive at regular intervals. Train services to vacation resorts such as the seaside town of Mar del Plata and the southern city of Bariloche are perhaps the most popular and are still widely used by travelers during the holiday season. Fares are relatively inexpensive and early booking is recommended, particularly in summer. For those with more time on their hands and a penchant for off-the-beaten-track experiences, the Tren de las Nubes ("Train of the Clouds") follows a route of breathtaking scenery across the northern Andes.

BUSES
Colectivos

Buses, commonly known as *colectivos*, are one of the most popular means of transportation in Argentina. In large cities there are many different lines, with Buenos Aires having 144; they are clearly numbered and easily distinguishable, as most lines have distinctive colors and designs. Ticket machines are located on the bus as you board. It is necessary to have change ready to pay the fare. There is a prepaid travel card system (*tarjeta SUBE*) that can be used on buses, trains, subways, and even to make payment at road tolls. These offer a cashless alternative and can be

purchased at dedicated SUBE outlets or ordered online. They can be topped up at cashpoints, through online banking, or at SUBE automatic kiosks.

In Buenos Aires there is a special bus service known as *diferencial*. These buses offer more comfortable seats and air-conditioning (although some standard buses are equipped with air conditioning too), and the number of passengers is limited to the number of seats. The routes they serve are normally more direct; the bus will only stop for passengers to alight and will only allow passengers on if there are empty seats. Not all lines offer this service.

Bus drivers are proud of their vehicles and many of them display ornate decorative objects— hanging plastic dice, flashing gearshift knobs, decorated rearview mirrors—and keep their buses very clean. Smoking is not permitted, and although eating is not explicitly forbidden it will be frowned upon and one might be asked to refrain from doing it.

Bus stops are located at regular intervals and one normally boards the bus by the front door and alights by the rear door. When one is ready to alight, the driver can be alerted via a bell located above the rear door.

A network of dedicated bus lanes known as Metrobus operates in Buenos Aires, offering covered bus shelters and travel information. The system operates on selected main avenues, although it is being extended to cover a wider area. Not all buses operate in these lanes and while the system has helped to ease congestion not all buses follow the Metrobus route its entire length

Long-Distance Coaches

The long-distance coach service in Argentina is quite good and there is a wide network of routes from Buenos Aires to all the other provinces as well as to neighboring countries, mainly Uruguay, Paraguay, and Brazil. As with some *colectivos*, coaches offer a standard service and a slightly better option (*diferencial*). The former is cheaper—seats are not guaranteed and do not have air-conditioning or heating, which given the extreme temperatures to be found in Argentina is something travelers should bear in mind. The latter option is more expensive but well worth it, particularly for long journeys. It offers comfortable reclining seats and in some cases flat beds for long-distance travel, air-conditioning, and heating. Many have an on-board service offering snacks and drinks.

Coach services depart from Buenos Aires Bus Terminal (Terminal de Buenos Aires) near Retiro rail station. There are over 140 coach lines operating from this terminal, and tickets can be purchased on level three of the building.

TAXIS

As in most large cities, taxis are common and are an easy and relatively cost-effective way of getting around. To avoid risk it is advisable to note the license plate and observe the driver (see page 133 below). In Buenos Aires there are over 32,000 registered taxis, making it easy to find one. Taxis are black with a yellow roof and display their license number on the doors in yellow letters. Taxis circulate day and night in the city of Buenos Aires and can be hailed anywhere in the street. The cost of the journey is metered, with the amount payable shown on the meter. Tipping is usually done by rounding up the fare. As in many places there are a few drivers who might try to take advantage of potentially unsuspecting visitors. Things to be aware of are longer routes, counterfeit notes (especially at night), and switching bank notes for ones of a lower value.

Radio taxis must be ordered by telephone and will collect the passenger at the agreed upon address. This is a safer alternative, particularly if you are traveling late at night.

Remises

Remises are privately owned vehicles akin to minicabs in the UK. The price of the journey is fixed in advance—this ensures a slightly better service and that the driver will take the most direct route to the passenger's destination. The *remise* is normally slightly dearer than a taxi—prices are usually verbally agreed upon—and is frequently used for journeys to and from the airport.

The use of remises has become a preferred option for many and is probably recommended over a taxi as it is considered safer.

THE METRO

Buenos Aires has an extensive underground network, the oldest in Latin America; this is still

evident in some of the rolling stock, which is not as modern as some of the networks in other countries. The metro is referred to as the *subterráneo*, or *subte* for short, and consists of five lines (named A to E) serving eighty stations across its 29 miles (46 kilometers) of network. Although perhaps not the most comfortable way to get around Buenos Aires, as it can be noisy and quite hot in summer, it is quick and efficient and is used by over a quarter of a million people each year.

The *subte* runs from Monday to Saturday from 6:00 a.m. to 11:00 p.m., and Sunday from 8:00 a.m. to 10:00 p.m. Tickets are one fixed price irrespective of the length of the journey and can be purchased at stations. There are also travel cards available; these are *Subtepass*, for one or more journeys, and *Subtecard*, which can be renewed or extended by direct debit to one's credit card.

BOATS

There is a good ferry service between Argentina and Uruguay. The largest company is Buquebus, offering daily services between Buenos Aires and the cities of Colonia and Montevideo and the Uruguayan seaside resort of Punta del Este. Although relatively costly, this service is fast and efficient, with a modern fleet of boats able to carry both passengers and cars. This option reduces the length of the journey to Uruguay should you decide to go by car.

DRIVING

Car rental in Argentina can be expensive, although it does offer a great amount of flexibility. There are a number of car rental companies, including the major international ones (Avis, Hertz, and Europcar) as well as local firms. These can be found in most cities and popular tourist destinations. Visitors can use their country's driver's license, although it is highly advisable to obtain an international one. Drivers must be eighteen years old or over.

Expressways are privately run in Argentina, so their use is not free; there are toll booths along the way. Expressways are well maintained and are usually quite wide, particularly near major cities, but they tend to become less reliable further away from those cities. There are many gas stations along the expressways, but for long journeys, particularly on off-expressway country roads, service stations might be harder to find. It is therefore sensible to fill the tank before leaving the expressway. In Argentina, gasoline is known as *nafta*.

Country roads tend to be old, poorly maintained, and often badly signposted.

Parking

It is always best to park in a parking lot (*playa de estacionamiento*), which is usually supervised. Street parking is allowed, but drivers are strongly advised to make sure they are legally parked. Tow trucks (*grua*) and clamps (*cepo*) are in operation in main cities.

RULES OF THE ROAD

A certain amount of bravado is required to drive in Argentina. Sadly, many basic rules are not followed and Argentina has one of the highest accident rates in the world. Visitors are advised to stay below the speed limit and follow the highway code. Drivers tend to be short-tempered and can be quite aggressive— the horn is constantly used, and bus drivers rule the roads with their rather discourteous driving habits. Some rules:

- The wearing of seat belts is compulsory, although the rule is not always followed.
- Traffic drives on the right.
- In built-up areas the speed limit is 25 mph (40 kmph) on small roads and 37 mph (60 kmph) on large avenues. On expressways the speed limit is 75 mph (120 kmph), but it is only 50 mph (80 kmph) on main roads.
- Left turns at traffic lights are not allowed unless there is a filter light with an arrow.
- Headlights should be on during the daytime.
- There are hefty penalties for driving under the influence of alcohol.

Driving in Buenos Aires

Despite its broad avenues and synchronized traffic lights, traffic in Buenos Aires can be chaotic, and drivers tend to be more aggressive than in smaller towns and rural areas.

Traffic is disorderly and the driving attitude is very defensive, with little if any respect for other drivers and even less for pedestrians. Driving in

Buenos Aires demands extreme caution and quick thinking, as advance warning and signaling are not commonplace.

Rules of the road are ignored more often than not, particularly red traffic lights late at night, as a result of the rise in robberies. Driving is thus not recommended for the motoring faint of heart.

Driving Abroad

From Argentina, one can easily drive to neighboring countries. There are expressways that cover long distances to Chile, Bolivia, Paraguay, Brazil, and Uruguay, although the latter is more easily reached by ferry (see page 126 above), and with a significant reduction in journey length. The ferry is also recommended if you are driving to Brazil.

There are border controls where a passport and visa (if required) should be produced, together with your vehicle registration documents and insurance policy. It is advisable to check with the authorities for the most up-to-date requirements. The Automovil Club Argentino provides information on most driving-related services, including roadside assistance and insurance.

FLYING

There are thirty-two airports used for passenger flights. The main airport is Ezeiza Airport (EZE), located about 22 miles (34 kilometers) from the city center. This is where most international flights arrive and depart, offering frequent services to Europe, the USA, and various Latin

American destinations. It is worth remembering that departing passengers have to pay an airport tax, equivalent to 5 percent of the price of the ticket, and a security tax in addition to that.

For air travel from Buenos Aires to other provinces within the country, or to Uruguay and some Brazilian destinations, there is a regular and frequent schedule from Aeroparque Jorge Newbery (AEP), the airport for domestic and regional flights located by the banks of the River Plate. There are more than 400 flights operating daily; most routes are operated by Aerolineas Argentinas (AR), the main national airline, although other, smaller airlines offer scheduled services to selected destinations. Aeroparque, as it is normally referred to, is conveniently located near the city center with easy access. Visitors are advised to take only licensed taxis or *remises* to the airport.

London in Argentina
The land upon which Jorge Newbery Airport is built was reclaimed from the River Plate and filled with rubble from the bombing of London in the Second World War. The ships that transported grain and cereals from Argentina to Europe during the war had to carry some ballast on their way back. It was this ballast that was used to fill the reclaimed land.

CYCLING
There are ample opportunities for cycling around the country. Mountain biking has become

increasingly popular, with the south of the country, near Bariloche, and the national parks being visited by many enthusiasts every year.

HEALTH AND INSURANCE

Pharmacists will dispense most medications, with many of them staying open all night. A list of pharmacies that are *de turno*—open all night, based on a rotation system—is normally displayed outside or on the window. Some medicines that might require a prescription in other countries may be sold over the counter in Argentina.

The state of the national health service in Argentina reflects the prevailing economic crisis and lack of investment. The medical profession in Argentina is still very highly regarded and of a high standard, however, particularly in the private sector. Private medical insurance is more than strongly recommended. Unlike many countries, the private sector allows patients to make an appointment directly with a specialist rather than having to be referred by their family doctor, although the latter practice is still recommended.

WHERE TO STAY

Argentina has always been an attractive tourist destination, and the provision of accommodation has developed considerably over the last few years. There are options to meet all budgets, ranging from modest one- or two-star establishments to first-class international hotels. The major international chains are present, along with independent luxury

hotels such as the Alvear Palace in the elegant area of Recoleta in Buenos Aires, one of the top hotels in Latin America. From modern towers and nineteenth-century French architecture to simple rural hotels or *hosterias*, there is no shortage of accommodation.

Accommodation in popular vacation destinations such as seaside and ski resorts is usually of a good standard. Huts and cabins are very popular, particularly in the lake region in the south near the main ski resorts. They offer comfort and bucolic locations close to many national parks.

Residence inns (*apart-hotel*) are normally restricted to larger cities and are suitable for longer stays. Toward the lower end of the budget, bed and breakfast accommodation (*hostales*) is a good option for travelers wishing to explore local areas.

SECURITY

Argentinian cities are not as dangerous as those in other Latin American countries. Unfortunately this relative safety has been affected by the economic crises of the last few years, the rise in the activity of drug cartels, and gang violence, resulting in a sharp increase in both theft and violent crime. This is most evident in Buenos Aires, not only on account of its size and fast pace but also because of the widening gap between the rich and the poor. In a city where walking late at night once presented few problems, it is now advisable to take precautions. Be careful with belongings such as bags, purses, and cell phones, and do not draw attention to yourself by carrying valuable objects, at least visibly.

It is sensible to avoid dark, empty streets, walking alone at night, and generally putting oneself in a vulnerable position, as one would anywhere. It is not uncommon for beggars to approach tourists. The best policy is to ignore them and move away. It is not advisable to give them money, at the risk of being robbed, or to engage in arguments or conversation.

Sadly, the number of violent crimes has soared, and robberies (often at gunpoint), muggings, and kidnappings (particularly in taxis) have become more frequent. It is therefore important to pay attention before boarding a taxi, and it is recommended that visitors take only registered radio taxis in order to avoid risky situations.

Smaller cities and towns tend to be peaceful, safe places where life runs at a slower pace and people are hospitable, friendly, and welcoming.

chapter eight

BUSINESS BRIEFING

BUSINESS CULTURE

Business practices in Argentina vary according to the region. The fast-moving businesspeople of Buenos Aires will be more vociferous and have developed a sense of polychronism that can disconcert the more methodical northern Europeans. Timetables will be juggled around to fit priorities. By contrast, their counterparts from smaller provincial towns will be more self-effacing and appear to be less emotional. They will probably find the *Porteños* arrogant and slightly overbearing.

As in many other countries, who you know is more important than what you know. Knowing the right people to pull the right strings—a concept known as *acomodo* ("comfort")—can give the least likely candidate an excellent opportunity. Because of the emotional and personal involvement Argentinians have with work—as opposed to the more rational and competence-driven approach found elsewhere—those who have been offered a job by virtue of their connections (*acomodados*) will tend to enjoy a certain amount of latitude.

Argentina, like many other Latin cultures, is very bureaucratic in its business approach.

Expediency is not the foundation of business negotiations—rather, the opposite is true. Argentinians like to take their time and believe that almost any aspect of a contract can be renegotiated.

Like their Italian and Spanish ancestors, the Argentinians place more emphasis on personal relationships than on rules. They would rather do business with a friend than get down to the nuts and bolts of the legal aspects of a contract and neglect the personal side of the relationship. For the visitor who comes from a more formal context (in the Latin view, a colder approach), it is worth being prepared to consider the business scenario in terms of personal implications.

You will be more successful in business negotiations if you allow the time to build a relationship with your prospective partners and colleagues, where small talk on topics like football or current affairs will play a role, than if you try to stick to schedules and the letter of the law.

Leadership and Decision Making

Argentinian business culture is generally one in which seniority is directly proportional to length of service, titles are extensively used, and decisions are made almost exclusively at the top level. Despite this, a shift toward a more achievement-oriented structure has become more prevalent as globalization gains ground, particularly in international organizations.

Many of these organizations are adopting a management and leadership style closer to that found in the USA, where a wider cross-section of the company can be involved in the decision-making process. However, as in many Latin and Mediterranean cultures, the system is generally quite hierarchical—the boss (*el jefe*) is still the boss, and he or she (although still mostly he) should be treated with the appropriate deference.

As Argentinian people are still very family oriented, bosses will often take a more lenient attitude toward their staff's problems if those problems are family related. Unfavorable economic climates, sadly, have made organizations less ready to offer such leniency. The increased activity of trade unions has kept the senior management of many organizations in check. Strikes and picket lines are commonplace, as workers attempt to preserve their jobs.

Smaller Argentinian organizations typically have a little more latitude when it comes to employment policies and are less vulnerable to the effects of industrial action, although this is also changing as legislation starts to affect all areas of industry and commerce.

Superiors are still seen in a rather patriarchal light, and subordinates may turn to them for help in work-related and other issues. This is less evident in the large corporations but still very prevalent in smaller, family-run businesses.

Teamwork

The individualist mentality of the Argentinians is slowly giving way to a more cooperative approach. This is driven more by external market forces than by the Argentinians' own volition.

Teams have to be clearly directed if a successful outcome, or any outcome at all, is required. Argentinians as a people have traditionally been directed "from above," both politically and professionally. Empowerment and autonomy should be closely monitored, and sometimes teams might require a gentle push in order to achieve results.

Argentinians tend to be professional in their approach to work and are usually knowledgeable when it comes to their own core competencies and skills. However, one might end up with a team of individual experts who will collectively struggle to produce the synergy required for a result that matches their expertise.

Presentation and Listening Styles

As in most of the rather emotional Latin cultures, the Argentinian speaking/listening pattern can be disconcerting to a visitor more accustomed to being listened to uninterruptedly, with time for questions at the end. Interruptions are likely to occur, so a preprepared script for a presentation will probably not work. Argentinians will listen, however, and although they might convey the impression that they are thinking about what they are going to say next rather than taking in what the presenter is saying, this is normally a misconception.

Very rigid and formal presentations are not recommended; the approach should be professional yet relaxed. Don't be surprised if not all the participants arrive on time. The presentation will normally start when the most senior person arrives, and still you might find latecomers trickling in after it has started.

MEETINGS AND NEGOTIATIONS

Although many organizations require a certain command of English as a prerequisite, the reality is quite different when it comes to negotiating. Even if your counterpart speaks relatively good English, he or she might not feel comfortable enough to conduct a transaction in English where the stakes are higher than in, say, a presentation. On the other hand, the person on the Argentinian side with the right command of the language might not have the required seniority to negotiate or even take part. In these cases an interpreter is recommended, or ask your Argentinian counterpart for suggestions.

Once trust has been gained, mainly through small talk and perhaps some socializing, both parties will feel more at ease when it comes to discussing terms of business.

The Argentinians are less narrowly focused than other cultures (particularly the Americans and the Europeans) and negotiations might seem to go off at a tangent, with topics bordering on the irrelevant. It is perhaps best to let the meeting take its course, occasionally trying gently to get back on to the key issues if sidetracking has gone on too long. A hard sell approach is not recommended as it will be seen as pushy and neglecting the personal touch.

Presenting a series of clauses in a precise and logical manner is unlikely to fit the Argentinian model—Argentinians will consider the impact of the outcome from both a business and a personal point of view. The bottom line is not the be all and end all of business negotiations in Argentina.

Despite the lengthy nature of negotiations, a contract is only finalized when all terms have been agreed upon and the document has been signed. Be prepared for last-minute changes and amendments; Argentinians can be tough negotiators

ETIQUETTE

Greetings

Men normally greet each other with a handshake and a slight nod of the head. Women may do the same, sometimes shaking hands with both hands and kissing each other on the cheek (once). This has become common among men, who will kiss each other on the cheek, although this is normally restricted to close friends and relatives. Once acquainted, men might hug each other (*abrazo*).

Handshaking between men and women is seen as quite formal. It is therefore not uncommon for men and women to kiss each other on the cheek when greeting. Don't be surprised if greeted in this way by a member of the opposite sex.

The exchange of business cards does not follow any formal protocol, and one might not always receive one in return.

You or You?

Like many languages in the world, Spanish has two forms of the second person singular, which are selected according to how formally one has to address the other person.

It is worth mentioning one of the main differences in grammar between Argentinian Spanish (Castellano) and the language spoken in all other Spanish-speaking countries. While the informal variation of the second person is *tu* in all other countries, in Argentina it is *vos*. It is still common practice to address someone senior or a new business acquaintance using the more formal *usted* (equivalent to the French *vous* or the German *Sie*), unless the other person insists that he or she be addressed as *vos*. If in doubt opt for the more formal option, which is normally used by calling people by their surname (without the use of Mr. or Mrs.) while still using the more formal register.

Nowadays, particularly in shops and retail outlets, it is not uncommon for staff to address customers using the less formal register.

Punctuality

Punctuality is expected in business meetings, and a courtesy call will not go amiss if you are running late. However, you should not be surprised if the other party does not reciprocate. It is not uncommon to be kept waiting—and in many cases, the more senior the person, the longer you will be kept waiting. It is advisable to reconfirm appointments a few days before.

When invited to a meal, a reception, the theater, or a concert, punctuality is observed all around. However, arrival times for less formal social events like parties are largely perfunctory; one is expected to arrive much later than the stipulated time, to the extent that arriving on time is considered impolite.

If punctuality is necessary in certain cases, the time will be emphasized with the qualifying expression *en punto* (on the dot). In such circumstances, you should not be late.

Office Dress and Etiquette

Argentinians place special emphasis on looks and appearance. They are stylish and fashionable, following the trends set by Italian and French fashion designers. Buenos Aires in particular has a very European outlook, and this is reflected in the way people dress. Dark suits for men and white blouses with suits or skirts for women are still the standard business attire. Casual Friday policies and an informal approach to business dress do not go over well.

Ironically, this formality is counterbalanced by the extroverted nature and openness of the Argentinians. The formality of e-mails and letters can be effectively replaced by a friendly chat over a cup of coffee. Argentina is a country where the tools for relationship building are readily available and should not be disregarded if you want to speak to the right person.

BUSINESS AND SOCIAL MEALS

Gastronomy is a key part of the Argentinian lifestyle, both from a social and business perspective, and the standard of their food is something Argentinians are quite rightly proud of.

Business meals are commonplace and are normally held in the evening after working hours. If you are the host, payment should be arranged in advance where possible. Otherwise you should insist on paying when the bill arrives. When summoning the waiter, do so by raising your hand, never by snapping your fingers. Although they are present on many tables, the use of toothpicks is ill advised, as is blowing one's nose at the table.

It is worth remembering that taxes on imported goods can be very high. Bear this in mind when ordering imported drinks, particularly as a guest, unless your host orders the drink in question.

GIFT GIVING

Argentina is not a country of lavish corporate gift giving, but one where a favor or *gauchada* is perhaps a preferred and more useful option. Expensive gifts might be construed as bribes and would put the receiver in an awkward position.

It is best to avoid personal items of clothing such as ties and shirts in order to avoid affronting the recipient's sense of style. Confine gifts to more neutral items. If one is given a gift it should be opened there and then and appreciation shown. It is still good practice to send flowers to one's hostess if

one is invited for dinner.
Pastries (*masitas*), generally
served with coffee after a
meal, or chocolates are also
suitable alternatives.

BODY LANGUAGE

You will realize almost immediately that the
outgoing personality of the Argentinians is
complemented by a rich-sounding language
and very visible body language. It is usual for two
parties to sit opposite each other and the host
will, in many cases, usher the guest to their seat.

During business meetings, the use of gestures
should be controlled; it is likely that as the
meeting progresses body language will relax.
Eye contact should be maintained.

When it comes to personal space, as we have
seen, Argentinians tend to stand closer to each
other when communicating. While this may
make some visitors uncomfortable, avoid
backing away as this will send the wrong signals.
Argentinians also go in for much more physical
contact—hugs, kissing, handshaking, and placing
a hand on a person's back when inviting them in
or asking them to go first, are normal behavior.

WOMEN IN BUSINESS

While Argentina is still a male-dominated
culture, women are gaining ground. Although
women have had great political influence in the
past, their standing in both politics and business

has become much more visible over the last couple of decades. They seldom hold public positions of power in business, but may exercise considerable control behind the scenes. Women from established wealthy families have occupied important positions within the field of business and the arts.

Foreign women should state their position, particularly the level of seniority within the company they represent, from the outset. They should not experience problems conducting business in Argentina as long as they remain professional in manner and dress and sensitive to local norms.

chapter nine

COMMUNICATING

THE LANGUAGE

Spanish is the third-most widely spoken language in the world after Mandarin and English. However, the Castilian Spanish of Argentina differs widely in accent and to a certain extent in its grammar and vocabulary from that spoken elsewhere (see page 140 above).

The European Spanish sound "z" (pronounced as "th" in thumb) is not used at all in Latin American Spanish from Mexico to Argentina. Argentinians pronounce the "ll" differently from all other Spanish-speaking countries. The "ll" in the word *lluvia* (the Spanish for rain), for instance, is pronounced as the "s" in "leisure," whereas in all other Spanish-speaking countries it would be pronounced as the "y" in "you." The same applies to the pronunciation of the letter "y." These two sounds are unmistakably Argentinian, although some Uruguayans, due to their proximity, have adopted them.

Another characteristic of the language, particularly in Buenos Aires, is the aspirated "s." This is used when the letter "s" precedes another consonant. Thus the "s" sound in words like *aspecto* (aspect), *fosforo* (a match, or the element phosphorous), and *estacion* (station) sounds more like the "h" in "handbook."

There are several noticeably different accents within the country, the Spanish of the northern provinces sounding closer to that of the Paraguayans, and that of the northwest being reminiscent of the Spanish of Bolivia. People from Córdoba have perhaps the most distinctive accent to the untrained ear in Spanish, as they tend to lengthen their vowels in such a manner that it sounds almost as though they are singing.

The *Porteños* tend to speak louder and faster than the rest of the population, in the belief that their speech is more sophisticated than those of the other provinces.

The general level of sound is much higher than it is in, say, the USA or the UK. It is not uncommon for visitors to think that people are shouting or raising their voice. This is not the case; if it were, the difference in body language and decibels would be a sure sign of ire even to those with no command of the language.

English is studied at school, but not in great depth; it is therefore not widely spoken outside certain circles, and if you should need to ask for directions in the street or communicate with a cab driver, for example, a minimum knowledge of Spanish is recommended.

Learning Spanish
Spanish is spoken by almost 300 million people worldwide. The differences between Argentinian

Spanish and other forms of the language will not prevent Argentinian Spanish speakers from communicating with people from other Hispanic countries, in much the same way as a distinctive US accent will not impede communication with an Australian.

Spanish, irrespective of its accent, is a language that is rich in vocabulary, expressive in sound, and not as difficult to learn as other languages. There are some difficult points that take time to master, particularly as there are two forms of the verb "to be" (*ser* and *estar*).

There are several schools of Spanish for foreigners in Argentina. Daily life will provide learners with an ideal opportunity to learn, as the gregarious Argentinians will be happy to engage in conversation and will be more than indulgent if your tenses or your noun and article genders are not totally accurate.

A Few Language Tips

The Spanish alphabet consists of twenty-six letters, although the letter "w" is only used in words of foreign origin. Some scholars might argue that the "*ch*" and the "*ll*" should be considered as separate letters, but dwelling on this would be outside the scope of this book.

Spanish is pronounced as written, with vowel sounds being pure (i.e., one sound only per vowel, unlike English, where the "u" in "huge" consists of two sounds).

a Pronounced as in "have."
c Pronounced soft as in "city" before e or i and hard as in "can" before any other letter.

ch Always pronounced as in "chair."

e Pronounced as the first "I" in "India."

g Pronounced as the "ch" in "loch" before i or e and hard as in "*go*" in all other cases.

h This is a silent consonant with no exceptions. The aspirated "h" sound is not used for this letter in Spanish.

i Pronounced as the "ee" in "sheep."

j Pronounced as the "ch" in "loch."

ll Pronounced as the "s" in "leisure." This is one of the main sounds that differentiates Argentinian Spanish from most other forms of the language.

ñ Pronounced as in "new."

r "R's are sometimes rolled and on occasions flicked. Double "r's are always rolled.

s Pronounced as in "see." However, Argentinians tend to drop the "s" sound for an aspirated "h" sound, particularly when it appears in the middle of a word. The extent to which this is done varies regionally. Most people will pronounce the Spanish for "listen to me" (*escuchame*) with an aspirated "s."

t As in all Latin languages, the "t" is not aspirated; i.e., it is formed by placing one's tongue slightly between the front teeth, thus avoiding the characteristic hissing English "t" sound.

u Always pronounced as the "oo" in "room."

v Strictly speaking, this is pronounced in the same way as in English. However, Argentinians tend to pronounce it in the same way as a soft "b"; i.e., by placing both lips together but still allowing some air to

pass through them. It is not uncommon for
people to refer to "v" as "*b corta*" ("short b")
and "b" as "*b larga*" ("long b"), using the
actual "b" sound in both cases!

y This is another characteristic Argentinian
sound. Similar to the "ll" sound, it is
pronounced as the "s" in "leisure."

z This is pronounced the same way as an s.
The characteristic European "th" (as in
"thumb") sound is not used in Argentina,
or indeed in other Latin American forms of
the language.

As a result of slightly different grammar,
some verbs are stressed differently than in
European Spanish. The accent (´) placed above
a word indicates that the syllable carries the
stress (only one can appear in a word).

The second person singular and plural
of verbs are where the difference in stress is
normally found. While a Spanish person will
say "*tu hazlo,*" meaning "you do it," with a stress
on the first syllable, Argentinians will say "*vos
hacelo*" with the stress on the second syllable.

This being said, any foreigner in the process
of learning the language will be taught the
"classical grammar" used in Spain. However,
the metalanguage (i.e., the language used to
teach this so-called "classical grammar") will be
Castilian Spanish. Saying "*tu tienes*" for "you
have" instead of its Castilian equivalent of "*vos
tenés*" will not only be forgiven but will also not
impede communication in any way.

"*Che*": What Does It Mean?

This ubiquitous, informal, very singular three-letter word is used to convey a variety of messages. Its origin dates back to the language spoken by the Mapuche tribe, in which it meant "man." Its most common use is to informally call someone: "*Che, dónde vas?*" ("Hey, where are you going?") It can also be used to emphasize a question: "*Que hacés, che?*" (Loosely translated as "So, what are you doing?", also used as a very informal greeting.) It can even, with the right intonation, show emotions that range from slight disapproval to righteous indignation, normally pronounced with a long "*e*" sound at the end.

The use of "*che*" is one of the hardest aspects of the Argentinian language to teach in a formal educational setting. Its proper use can only be learned through practice and exposure to the language. The most important thing to remember is that it is informal in its use and should not be used in business contexts, in much the same way that English speakers would avoid using the interjection "hey" in similar formal situations.

What's in a Nickname?

Ernesto Guevara, the famous leader of the Cuban revolution, was nicknamed "Che" by the Cubans as a result of his distinctive Argentinian accent and his frequent use of the word "che."

Most Spanish nouns ending in "o" are masculine and most ending in "a" are feminine.

Slang
Lunfardo, as slang is called in Argentina, also varies regionally. Buenos Aires slang, normally associated with tango as the lyrics of that style of music feature many slang words, contains a high proportion of Italianized words. "*Laburo*" is the slang for "work" ("*lavoro*" in Italian), to name but one very frequently used example. While the younger generations have developed their own form of slang, the Italian ancestry so dominant in the population of Argentina, particularly Buenos Aires, yet again manifests itself through slang.

FACE-TO-FACE CONVERSATION
Argentina is the place to go to for those who enjoy the art of conversation. Remember, the overall decibel level of the talkative *Porteños* is much higher than that of Northern Europeans. Conversations may sound agitated and hostile to the unaccustomed ear, but in most cases this is simply the characteristically Argentinian way of speaking, usually accompanied by quasi-choreographic displays of body language.

In cafés, restaurants, and even public squares, particularly in Buenos Aires, it is always possible to witness the Argentinians engaging in some form of debate. Everyone claims to have the solution to the country's economic, political, or social problems, making debates of this nature quite intense, yet friendly.

A FEW USEFUL PHRASES

Hola Hello (also used when answering the phone)

Buen día/Buenos días Good morning (literally, Good day)

Buenas tardes Good afternoon

Buenas noches Good evening/Good night

Como estás? Como andás? Como te va?
How are you? (informal)

Como le va? Como está? How are you? (formal)

Por favor Please

Gracias Thank you

De nada You're welcome

Perdón Excuse me/Sorry

Salud! Cheers/Bless you (as when someone sneezes)

Chau/Hasta luego Good-bye

Mañana Tomorrow

Hoy Today

Ayer Yesterday

La semana que viene Next week

Topics and Taboos

For the visitor it is wise to refrain from making comments about the current situation in Argentina. Argentinians are happy to criticize their own country quite vociferously but do not take well to outside criticism. Topics such as the Falklands War should be avoided; if asked your opinion on the war (quite unlikely, more than three decades on), it is best to be as noncommittal as possible while showing sympathy toward those who perished during the conflict.

The subjects of Perón, his wives, government, or policies are best avoided. Care should be taken as there is no middle ground here—feelings on Perón, whether positive or negative, will be very strong. Admittedly more popular with the working classes, even idolized by many, he also has occasional sympathizers among the better educated. This could perhaps be because the individual holds a position within the government, or has had previous associations with the party. It is worth bearing in mind that, at the time of writing, the Justicialista (Peronist) Party is in power.

Argentinians do not like to be challenged and will tend to adopt a defensive attitude, while managing to reply with a smile on their face. Delving too deeply into the rationale of a particular piece of legislation or the "why" of the status quo is not advisable unless, of course, you know the other party quite well.

Other areas to be avoided, at least when talking to new acquaintances, are racism, religion, and other personal or sensitive topics such as the Nazi war criminals living in Argentina. These issues may be too close for comfort, and may elicit comments or opinions that are likely to offend visitors from more multicultural and multiracial societies.

In line with the Argentinians' pride in their European ancestry, comparisons with other Latin American countries should be avoided. This is particularly true of Brazil, where there is still a slight feeling of animosity, although perhaps more on behalf of the Brazilians, who see the Argentinians as arrogant and abrupt.

Silence

Silence is not something with which most Argentinians feel comfortable. This is perhaps more true of city dwellers than those living in remote rural areas.

The Argentinian pattern of conversation is almost uninterrupted, giving the impression that people are already thinking about what to say next while you are talking to them. This fast pace of exchange is hard to keep up with at first, but most visitors will be given grace and their hosts will slow down the flow of their speech to accommodate them.

Swearing

Swearing has become more commonplace in Argentina. While no swearing used to be heard on radio and television, this has changed with the arrival of democracy. Nevertheless, even in today's more relaxed society, the use of unseemly language among the young is frowned on by many of the older generation. Swearing is still widely viewed as unnecessary and as showing a lack of refinement, and visitors are strongly encouraged to avoid it.

Argentinian swearwords tend to allude to one's maternal ancestry, and although these are often used inoffensively—perhaps to emphasize a feeling, not always of anger or discontent—it will take time and a certain amount of restraint on behalf of the visitor to get used to this.

Humor

Argentinians are always ready for a good laugh, generally at somebody else's expense. Their humor is less subtle than British humor, which is often not thought funny. Understatement is not part of Argentinian humor, although situational visual comedy is. Irony and wit are key elements in the humor of Buenos Aires, which makes good use of the richness of the region's language.

Visitors might be taken aback to find their clothes, weight, or accent becoming the butt of jokes. There is no irreverence or disrespect intended, so it is best just to accept this.

Argentinians are not very good when it comes to laughing at themselves and would much rather pick on a different group of people. The Spanish, notably the Galicians (*Gallegos*), have historically been the butt of many jokes. Sadly, the definition of Galicians has extended to anyone speaking with a Spanish (from Spain) accent.

THE PRESS

There is no shortage of newspapers in Argentina. Every province has its own local newspaper in addition to the main national press. The leading newspapers are *El Clarín*, renowned for its content and classified ads, *Página 12*, and *Ambito Financiero* for general news and news on financial markets. The main serious newspapers are *La Nación*, *La Razón*, and *La Prensa*.

The *Buenos Aires Herald* is the only newspaper printed in English, and has been in circulation

since 1876. It covers both national and international news as well as details on entertainment, dining, and shopping. Foreign newspapers can be bought in selected newsdealers in city centers; the *International Herald Tribune, Wall Street Journal*, and *Financial Times* will be one or two days old as the distribution logistics have to contend with long distances and time differences.

TELEVISION AND RADIO

Television is an integral part of Argentinian life. Eating in front of the TV and having it perpetually on, whether or not it is being watched, is still common practice in very many households.

There are five VHF/UHF channels: Channel 13 (Artear), Channel 11 (Telefe), Channel 2 (America TV), Channel 9 (Libertad), and Channel 7 (ATC), the state television channel. Most films and foreign programs are dubbed (rather than using subtitles),

unlike those shown in the cinema, where subtitles still prevail (see pages 102–3).

In addition to this, the satellite and cable-TV network extends to almost all the country, giving access to international channels such as the BBC and CNN.

There are many radio stations broadcasting in both AM and FM, with programs to suit every audience.

MAIL

The main postal company is the Central Post (Correo Central), which works reasonably well. There are other private companies such as Oca and Servicor offering these services, with branches across the country.

Using standard delivery, a letter can take from ten to fifteen days from Argentina to the UK, and slightly less to the USA. If sending postcards it is best to send these in an envelope, rather than just addressing on the back. Special delivery services and international courier companies like DHL and FedEx are widely available. Letters must be properly addressed with the name of the addressee, full address, and zip or postcode.

TELEPHONE

The local telephone system is not as good as that of many other countries, although it is systematically improving. The international dialing code for Argentina is 54, the code for Buenos Aires is 11, and all numbers start with a 4. Long-distance area codes vary according to the region: 1 for Buenos Aires and the surrounding area, 2 for the south of the country, and 3 for the north of the country. The prefix for long-distance calls is 0, followed by the area code, and for international calls the prefix is 00 followed by the country code.

Local and international calls can be made from public telephones, telephone centers (*telecentros*), and telephone offices (*locutorios*). Calls can also be made from hotels but, as in most countries, there will be a surcharge of up to 30 percent.

In the center of Buenos Aires and larger cities there is no shortage of public telephones. Most of these are card operated; cards can be obtained from *telecentros* or *kioskos*. Very few public telephones take coins.

There are plenty of *locutorios* and *telecentros* in large cities. These are more comfortable than talking on a public phone in the street, and one is charged on a pay-as-you-talk basis with a display

indicating the duration of the call and the cost so far. There are two call rates, with the lower rates operating from 10:00 p.m. to 8:00 a.m., Monday to Friday, and from 1:00 p.m. on Saturday to 8:00 a.m. on Monday.

People will answer calls by saying "*Hola*" (with the stress on the first syllable); internal calls (within a company) might be answered with a simple "*Si*" with a rising intonation.

Some useful telephone numbers are listed below. Calls will be taken in Spanish.

Ambulance 107	
Police and Fire Department 101	
Information Service/Directory Inquiries 110	
National Operator 19	
International Operator 000	

Cell Phones

To call cell phones in Buenos Aires you must dial the prefix 15. Roaming is available on some international networks, but you are strongly advised to check the roaming rates with your provider before departure in order to avoid unexpectedly high bills.

THE INTERNET

As in most countries in Latin America, e-mail and Internet services are widely used in Argentina, with broadband high-speed Internet access in many homes. Internet cafés (or cybercafés) are mainly found in large cities, offering high-speed Internet access at quite reasonable prices. The *telecentros* also offer similar services, in addition to the telephone service previously mentioned. Most reputable hotels offer Internet access to their guests, in many cases free of charge.

The infrastructure in small rural communities and towns in the interior of the country might not be as advanced, and Internet access (if available) will probably be by means of a dial-up connection.

It is relatively easy, therefore, for visitors to check their e-mail through a Web browser in any of the above places. Both Yahoo and Google have a localized Spanish version of their portals for Argentina, thus offering the option to search for information pertinent to the country.

CONCLUSION

Argentina sometimes seems like a European country that has somehow been misplaced in South America. It is a huge and appealing country, whose importance in the global economy as a producer of food has enabled it to survive the direst of economic crises. Argentina is a crippled giant, waiting for the right moment to reveal its potential and perhaps relive its former glory as one of the richest countries in the world.

The Argentinians never cease to astound visitors with the sophistication of the *Porteños* and the candidness and laid-back style of the rural population. Argentina is still a place where, despite ongoing difficulties, friendship is a key ingredient in getting things done. It is a country that has lived for today and looks as though it will continue to do so, its people having developed an art of extemporization that is probably second to none. The Argentinians' identity is still very southern European, and their exuberant way of life will charm and engage even the most reticent and self-effacing visitors.

From a business perspective, the latitude that Argentinians allow themselves when it comes to punctuality and the amount of small talk that normally precedes getting down to business is counterbalanced by their openness and hospitality, and a wish to show the best they have to offer.

The Argentinians are a vibrant and resilient people, proud of their success in recovering from repressive dictatorial regimes, and whose *joie de vivre* and generosity of spirit can be contagious. They will be happy to teach you about their country, their people, their traditions, and their rich and colorful language. Here is a society where making friends is part of daily life, and where becoming part of that way of life will prove to be an exciting, enriching, and unique experience.

Further Reading

Bernhardson, Wayne, and Sandra Bao. *Lonely Planet Guide: Argentina, Uruguay and Chile*. Hawthorn, Victoria; Oakland, California; London; and Paris: Lonely Planet Publications, 2002.

Foster, David William, et al. *Culture and Customs of Argentina*. Westport, Connecticut: Greenwood Press, 1998.

Goñi, Uki. *The Real Odessa: How Perón Brought the Nazi War Criminals to Argentina*. London: Granta Books, 2003.

Hennessy, Huw (ed.). *Argentina, Insight Guide*. London and New York: APA Publications GmbH & Co. Verlag, 2002.

Lewis, Colin M. *Argentina: A Short History*. Oxford: Oneworld, 2002.

Nouzeilles, Gabriela. *The Argentina Reader: History, Culture, Politics*. Durham and London: Duke University Press, 2002.

Spanish. A Complete Course. New York: Living Language, 2005.

In-Flight Spanish. New York: Living Language, 2001.

Fodor's Spanish for Travelers (CD Package). New York: Living Language, 2005.

Useful Web Sites

www.argentina.com
Portal with various links and information about travel in
Argentina.

www.thebuenosairesherald.com
On-line version of the English-language newspaper.

english.buenosaires.com
On-line guide to the city of Buenos Aires.

www.sectur.gov.ar
Official site of the national tourist office.

www.expat-today.com/country_file/argentina/
Useful facts for those relocating to Argentina.

www.thesuburbanplayers.com/
Web site of the English-speaking theater group in Buenos Aires.

www.escapeartist.com/argentina6/tournet.htm
Portal with links to various sites containing information about
living in Argentina.

Index

Acknowledgments

The author has drawn on the work of many fellow researchers, including Penny Carté and Chris Fox's *Bridging The Culture Gap* (London: Kogan Page, 2004); Ricardo Luis Molinari's *Buenos Aires 4 Siglos* (Buenos Aires: Tipográfica Editora Argentina, 1984); and Fons Trompenaars and Charles Hampden-Turner's *Riding the Waves of Culture* (London: Nicholas Brealey, 1997).

This book is dedicated to my wife, Sandra.